PROFESSOR S. N. DASGUPTA
Presidency College, Calcutta

HINDU MYSTICISM

SIX LECTURES

BY

S. N. DASGUPTA, M.A., Ph.D. (Cal.), Ph.D. (Cantab.)

Late Lecturer in the University of Cambridge, England. Late
Professor of Sanskrit, Chittagong College, Bengal.
Professor of Philosophy, Presidency College,
Calcutta. Author of "A History of
Indian Philosophy," "Yoga as
Philosophy and Religion."

(Norman Wait Harris Foundation Lectures, 1926)
Northwestern University
Evanston, Ill.

CHICAGO : : LONDON
THE OPEN COURT PUBLISHING CO.
1927

To

HIS EXCELLENCY

The Rt. Hon'ble Victor Alexander George Robert Bulwer-Lytton, Earl of Lytton P.C., G.C.S.I., G.C.I.E., Chancellor of The University of Calcutta and Governor of Bengal, India.

May it please your Excellency,

I know that your noble and cultivated soul will always be eager to receive with cordial hospitality the high ideals, thoughts and attainments of the people of any age and of any country, but more particularly of India, over the destinies of a part of which your excellency had to preside for some time.

Mine is a humble performance, but I feel extremely grateful to you that it was solely through the kind patronage of your excellency that I could avail myself of the opportunities that came and accept the invitations of many foreign universities, at one of which these lectures were delivered. Your generous courtesies, cordiality and sympathetic willingness to help will always endear your name to me, as it will do to many others. By associating this brief account of the mystics of India with your name I am only paying my tribute of respect to you for the high respect that you yourself have for the lofty ideals of humanity. I shall be glad if you will kindly accept this unworthy gift and sometimes think of India, her past greatness and future possibilities.

I remain your Excellency,
Loyally and sincerely yours,

Surendranath Dasgupta,
Presidency College,
Calcutta.

v

THE N. W. HARRIS LECTURES

were founded in 1906 through the generosity of Mr. Norman Wait Harris of Chicago, and are to be given annually. The purpose of the lecture foundation is, as expressed by the donor, "to stimulate scientific research of the highest type and to bring the results of such research before the students and friends of Northwestern University, and through them to the world. By the term 'scientific research' is meant scholarly investigation into any department of human thought or effort without limitation to research in the so-called natural sciences, but with a desire that such investigation should be extended to cover the whole field of human knowledge."

PREFACE

BOTH on the continent and in America, Hindus are associated with mysticism, but, so far as I know, the subject of Hindu mysticism has as yet received no systematic treatment, either in the way of general introduction, or in the way of a comprehensive account. The man in the street cannot, as a rule, distinguish between the lower and the higher forms of mysticism. He looks upon mysticism in general with some kind of superstitious awe or reverence, and he thinks of it as an obscure and supernatural method by which, in some unaccountable manner, miraculous feats may be performed or physical advantages reaped—departed spirits made visible, fortunes told, muscles developed, riches earned without effort, dangerous and incurable diseases cured by simple amulets or blessings, infallible prophesies made, and the like. I shall not say anything as to whether or not such phenomena are possible, for my present interest concerns not facts but beliefs. But whether or not the phenomena actually occur, they imply beliefs that there are short cuts to the attainment of advantages through mysterious, supernatural or miraculous powers undiscoverable by reason. I refer to this as inferior mysticism, because the purposes relate solely to the attainment of inferior mundane benefits. Distinguishable therefrom is the belief that the highest reality or the ultimate realisation and fulfilment (whatever may be their nature) cannot be attained by reason alone, but that there are other avenues to them, namely, the firm and steady control of will, the development of right emotions, or both combined, or by them both along with the highest functioning of reason. This is superior and true mysticism because it is directed to the liberation of the spirit and the attainment of the highest bliss.

Mysticism in Europe has a definite history. In spite of the variety of its types, it may roughly be described to refer to the belief that God is realised through ecstatic communion with Him. With the Islamic mystics, the Christian mystics, and the devotional mystics or bhaktas of India, the vision of God and His grace is attained through devotional communion or devotional rapture of various kinds. But in all these mystics, we find a keen sense of the necessity of purity of mind, contentment, ever alert striving for moral goodness, self-abnegation, and one-pointedness to God. There can be no true mysticism without real moral greatness. This mysticism should therefore be distinguished from a mere delusory faith that God often grants us a vision of Him or appears to us in dreams, or from a faith in the infallibility of the scriptures and so forth, for the latter are often but manifestations of credulity or of a tendency to believe in suggestions, and may often be associated with an inadequate alertness of critical and synthetic intellect.

I have defined mysticism as a belief or a view, but in reality it means much more than that. In the life of the true mystics, beliefs exert a great formative influence. They are no mere intellectual registrations of opinions or temporary experiences, but represent the dynamic, the dominant tone of their personality as it develops and perfects itself. Mysticism is not an intellectual theory; it is fundamentally an active, formative, creative, elevating and ennobling principle of life. I have not here taken note of poems or thoughts involving merely mystical beliefs but have touched only upon those which are the outward expressions of a real inner flowering of life in the persons of those who have tried to live a saintly life of mysticism.

Mysticism means a spiritual grasp of the aims and problems of life in a much more real and ultimate manner than is possible to mere reason. A developing life of mysticism means a gradual ascent in the scale of spiritual values, experience, and spiritual ideals. As such, it is many-sided in its development, and as rich and complete as life itself. Regarded from this point of view, mysticism is the basis of all religions—particularly of religion as it appears in the lives of truly religious men.

An acquaintance with Indian religious experience shows that there are types of religious and mystical experience other than that of an intimate communion with God. I have therefore made my definition of mysticism wider, so that it may include not only the Islamic, Christian, and the Bhakti forms of Indian mysticism but other types of Indian mysticism as well. I could not hope to give an exhaustive analysis or even a fairly comprehensive treatment of the chief features of the different types of Indian mysticism within the limits of these six lectures. I have therefore attempted only a brief general outline of some of the most important types, indicating their mutual relations, sometimes genetically and sometimes logically. I have omitted all reference to the connected metaphysical issues, as a comprehensive treatment of these philosophical problems may be found in my "A History of Indian Philosophy" (Cambridge University Press), the first volume of which has already been published and the other volumes are in the course of publication.

I have first described the sacrificial type of mysticism. This cannot in all its particulars be regarded as a mysticism of a superior order, but it develops many features of the higher types and marks the starting-point of the evolution of Indian mysticism. I have then discussed the four chief types of mysticism: the Upanishad, the Yogic, the Buddhistic and the Bhakti, though there are many branches of these particular types upon which I could not enter. I have mentioned some other minor types of mysticism. In addition there are some which are of a syncretistic nature, exhibiting elements of belief and duties of two or three distinct types of mysticism in combination. I could not present them all. The five main types that I have here described, however, may be regarded as funda-

mental; and, though very much more could have been
said in the way of elaboration and illustration, all their
striking characteristics have been briefly touched upon
and materials have largely been drawn directly from
the original sources. I hope that I may in the future
have an opportunity to take up the subject again and to
deal with it more elaborately.

Perhaps I should have entitled the present volume
"The Development of Indian Mysticism ." But the
word "Indian" might be misunderstood in America. I
have therefore selected "Hindu Mysticism," "Hindu"
standing for Indian. I have dropped the word "Development" to avoid any initial impression of forbidding
technicality. For similar reasons diacritical marks
have been omitted.

I now have the very pleasant duty of thanking the
Harris Foundation Lecture Committee which did me
the honour of asking me to deliver these lectures and
President Walter Dill Scott, Professor Edward L.
Schaub and Professor T. W. Koch, the Secretary of
the committee. Considering the high reputation of my
predecessors, who were outstanding scholars in their
respective branches of learning, I feel extremely dif-
fident about my own humble performance. I have received so much hospitality and kindness in America
that I shall always think of this great country with
appreciative enthusiasm and admiration. But I can
never express adequately my gratefulness and thanks
to Professor Edward L. Schaub, who was chiefly responsible for my invitations to the American Univer-

sities and who helped me so generously in seeing these lectures through the press, as well as in suggesting many changes of style and expression—to say nothing of his personal courtesies and cordiality which will always endear his name to me.

S. N. Dasgupta.

Calcutta, India, 1927.

ANALYTICAL TABLE OF CONTENTS

and truths discovered by reason should be attested
by reference to the Vedas.

11. Definition of mysticism.
12. Special features of sacrificial mysticism.
13. Development of sacrificial mysticism into substitution-meditations.
14. Some forms of substitution-meditations are found even now in India among certain sections of the people.
15. The development of substitution-meditations marks a new stage of advance towards the liberation of thought from the narrow limitations of sacrificial mysticism. Loose generalisation of thought made such an advance possible.
16. How the substitution-meditations contributed towards the development of the idea of Brahman, the supreme reality, as the identity of being, thought and bliss.
17. How the monotheistic Vedic hymns contributed towards the formation of the concept of Brahman.
18. The mysterious force of sacrifices and the idea of Brahman.
19. The dawn of a quest of Brahman.
20. Transition from the worship of deities to the highest realisation of truth and reality, the Brahman.
21. The rise of the Upanishad literature, which deals with the growth and development of the concept of Brahman, also called the Vedanta.

LECTURE II

1. Monotheistic hymn of Hiranyagarbha.
2. Though monotheistic passages are found in the sacrificial manuals, the emphasis is nevertheless almost wholly on the sacrificial system.
3. The science of Brahman is based wholly on the fact that the spiritual needs of man always tend to tran-

LECTURE III

tion of the mind necessary for the liberation of the spirit.

LECTURE IV

LECTURE I
SACRIFICIAL MYSTICISM

LECTURE I
SACRIFICIAL MYSTICISM

THE Hindus possess a body of sacred compositions called the Vedas. Of these there are four collections. Two of them comprise original hymns. The contents of the others consist largely of poems derived from the former two. The collections of original hymns, known as the Rig Veda and the Atharva Veda, include, respectively, 1028 original hymns of about 10600 stanzas and 731 hymns of about 6000 stanzas. All of these were kept in memory and transmitted by recitation and close memorizing on the part of teachers and pupils in an unbroken chain of early traditions from a time when writing was probably not known. The opinions of scholars vary greatly regarding the antiquity of this literature; some think that the hymns were composed about 6000 B. C. or at a still earlier date, while others think that they were composed about 1200 B. C. or 1000 B. C. The Vedic hymns are probably the earliest important religious documents of the human race. 1

The hymns of the Atharva Veda contain among other things descriptions of charms for curing diseases, prayers for long life and health, imprecations against demons, sorcerers and enemies, charms pertaining to women—to secure their love or arouse jealousy, and the like—charms for securing harmony and influence in an assembly, charms for securing the prosperity of household, fields, cattle, business, gambling, etc., charms in expiation of sins and defilement. The hymns of the Rig Veda, on the other hand, are often praises of various deities, who are frequently mere personifications of the different powers of nature, such as the rain-god, the wind-god, the fire-god, and the like. The prayers in these hymns are praises of the greatness and power, the mysterious nature, and the exploits of these deities, as well as prayers for various favors. Often the favors sought are of the nature of material blessings, such as long life, vigorous offspring, cattle and horses, gold, etc. Prayers for the advancement of the inner spiritual achievements of man, for righteousness or moral greatness, prayers expressing a passionate longing for the divine or a humble submission of the mind to the divine will are not so frequent. Most of these prayers were recited in the performance of certain prescribed rituals. Though from the praises of the gods one might infer that it was the gods who were supposed to bestow the benefits, it was in fact the complete set of ritualistic performances that was considered to be the cause of the showering of the benefits. It was supposed that these ritualistic performances when carried out in all their details, precisely and accurately, could by their joint and mysterious effect produce a mysterious something whereby the prayers were fulfilled. 2

I shall omit from my discussion the hymns of the Atharva Veda which deal only with spells, witchcraft and incantations. But while I take for examination those hymns of the Rig Veda which express beautiful ideas about the nature-deities and which voice personal requests for material comforts or for advantages, it should be understood that they also were chanted in connection with the performance of rituals and sacrifices. It is difficult to determine whether in the earliest period definite theories had been formulated regarding the intimate and indispensable connection between the chanting of these hymns of personal appeal and the performance of the rituals. But if we judge by the Vedic literature of the Brahmanas (probably composed shortly after the hymns, and later appended to them) which indicate authoritatively the place of these hymns in the ritualistic observances and specify what hymns were to be uttered under what ritualistic conditions and in what order or manner, it seems almost certain that the prevailing form of what is commonly called the Vedic religion may in strictness not be considered as a religion in the ordinarily accepted meaning of this term. Many of the ritualistic observances, or *yajna*, required the help of a large number of priests, and large quantities of butter, rice, milk, animals, etc. They had to be performed with the most elaborate details from day to day, for months together and sometimes even for ten or twelve years; and it was enjoined that all the observances should be performed in exact accordance with the prescriptions laid down in the Brahmana literature. Even the slightest inaccuracy or the most trifling inexactness would be sufficient to spoil the entire effect of the sacrifice. But if the sacrifices were performed with the strictest accuracy, then the material advantages for which they were performed were bound to come regardless of the good will or the ill will of the gods to whom the prayers were offered. Tvashtar had performed a sacrifice for the birth of a son who might kill Indra, but owing to a slight error in pronunciation the meaning of the prayer was changed and the sacrifice produced a son who was not a killer of Indra but of whom Indra was the killer. [3]

This idea of sacrifice is entirely different from anything found in other races. For with the Vedic people, the sacrifices were more powerful than the gods. The gods could be pleased or displeased; if the sacrifices were duly performed the prayers were bound to be fulfilled. The utterance or chanting of the stanzas of the Vedic hymns with specially prescribed accents and modulations, the pouring of the melted butter in the prescribed manner into the sacrificial fire, the husking of rice in a particular way, the making and exact placing of cakes, all the thousand details of rituals—often performed continuously for days, months and years with rigorous exactness—was called a *yajna* (frequently translated into English, "sacrifice"). All the good things that the people wanted, be it the birth of a son, a shower of rain, or a place of enjoyment in heaven, were believed to be secured through the performance of these sacrifices. It is possible that when these hymns were originally composed, they were but simple prayers to the deified powers of nature, or that they were only associated with some simple rituals.

But the evidence that is presented to us in the later Vedic and non-Vedic records containing descriptions of these sacrifices and discussions respecting their value, convinces us beyond doubt that it was the performance of these sacrifices, perfect in every detail in accordance with the dictates of the sacrificial manuals, the Brahmanas, that was believed to be capable of producing everything that a man could desire. A direct consequence of this apparently unmeaning necessity of strictest accuracy of ritualistic performances is a theory that came to be formulated and accepted in later periods, namely, that the sacrificial rites revealed such supernatural wisdom that they could not have been made by any one but were self-existent. It came to be held that the hymns of the Vedas, as well as the sacrificial manuals, were without authorship; that they existed eternally, prescribing certain courses of ritualistic procedure for the attainment of particular advantages and prohibiting certain undesirable courses of action. Consistently with the sacrificial theory it was also believed that the meanings of the hymns, so far as they described events or facts of nature or the exploits and the conduct of the gods were of a legendary character, that their true value consisted in the enjoining of particular courses of action or of dissuading people from other courses of action. 4

Religion in its ordinarily accepted sense means a personal relationship with some divine or transcendent person to whom we submit and to whom we pray for material advantages or for spiritual or moral enlightenment. But here was a belief in the divinity or the uncreatedness of a literature—the Vedas—which was believed to contain within itself the secret laws of the universe. Here there was a conception of commands, categorical in nature and external in character, without the least suggestion of any commander. Though these commands were supposed not to have emanated from any person, they may nevertheless in some sense be described as transcendent, for they were regarded as far above human wisdom. No reason could be given why a particular sacrificial performance should produce any particular kind of material advantage. There stand the commands—commands which had revealed themselves to the minds of the various sages, which had no beginning in time, which do not imply any commander, and which are absolutely faultless and unerring in their directions. 5

The sacrifices, thus, were supposed to possess a mysterious power capable of regulating and modifying the workings of the universe for the advantage of individuals; and the Vedic commands were thought to embody omniscience respecting the ways of the world. Though the repository of omniscience, the Vedas were not conceived as divulging to us their secrets but merely as providing a body of directions which, if followed, would give whatever advantages one craved in this life or the next. The sacrifices (*yajna*) or their mysterious powers, are called *dharma*, a term which in Indian vernaculars is often used wrongly to translate the English word "religion." The Vedic hymns, the priests, and the sacrifices are also called "the great" by the application of the term *brahman,* which in later Indian philosophy and religion had such a momentous history. 6

What we have described is no ordinary magic of spells and incantations, but a repository of the cosmic secrets and cosmic forces. These impersonal commands unite in them the concepts of an unalterable law and perfect omniscience; they imply therefore the possibility of reaping all the comforts of this life and of the after-life by submission to them and compliance with them. But they involve no law-giver, no divine person, no author of the universe or of the destinies of human beings who must be pacified, obeyed or loved, and by whose grace we receive the blessings of life. We can control our own destinies, and have whatever we may want, if we only follow the commands. There is no other mystery of life save this great mystery of the Vedic commands, and these are absolutely inscrutable. These commands do not teach ordinary laws of social life or of behavior toward our fellow-beings, or anything that we could discover by our own intelligence and wisdom. Neither do they teach us anything that we could learn by experience or reason. They give direction for the attainment of the good things of this life or of the after-life only in so far as the means thereto are absolutely undiscoverable by us. They are not a body of facts, but a body of commands and prohibitions. Yet they do not represent commands of the inner conscience or of the spirit within us; they do not give us any food for the spirit. They represent an objective and unalterable

law realistically conceived, and they relate to desires
for material comforts in this life or the life in heaven.
This concept gives us all the principal elements of religion except that of a divine person. The acceptance
of the blessings of this life as gifts from God, and a
sense of our duty to please Him by submission and
prayer are, therefore, not implied in this system of
Vedic sacrifices. What is implied is some great impersonal force which harmonises ourselves and our
destinies with the happenings and events of the world
of nature. Instead of God we find here a body of
commands which demand our obedience and reverence; but the source of their power and the secret of
their omniscient character and uncreatedness cannot
be determined by us through reason or experience.
But this ritualistic mysticism—if we may be permitted
thus to call it—must be distinguished from the simple
feelings and ideas that are found in the hymns themselves. In all probability the latter did not originally
imply the complicated ritualistic hypotheses of the later
period.   7

The forces of nature with their wonderful manifestations of inexplicable marvels appeared to the early
sages like great beings endowed with life and personality. They were treated at times as friendly, but again
as hostile. Sometimes the mystery of the natural
phenomena seemed stupifying in its psychological effect. The laws of nature were at that time unknown,
and there was no obstacle to the free flight of the
imagination. When the Vedic sage saw the sun pro-

ceeding in his upward and downward course through the sky he cried out in his wonder:

"Undropped beneath, not fastened firm, how comes it
That downward turned he falls not downward?
The guide of his ascending path,—who saw it?"[1]

The sage is full of wonder that "the sparkling waters of all rivers flow into one ocean without ever filling it." He perceives the unalterable course of the sun from day to day, and the succession of day and night, and he exclaims with delight: "Every day, in unceasing interchange with night and her dark wonders, comes the dawn with her beautiful ones to reanimate the worlds, never failing in her place, never in her time." Again, he is puzzled when thinking whither the shining ones of the sky disappear, and he cries forth in amazement:

"Who is it knows, and who can tell us surely
Where lies the path that leads to the Eternals?
Their deepest dwellings only we discover,
And hidden these in distant secret regions."

In how many hymns does the singer express his wonder that the rough red cow gives soft white milk. To the god Indra he cries:

"Grant me, O God, the highest, best of treasures,
A judging mind, prosperity abiding,
Riches abundant, lasting health of body,
The grace of eloquence, and days propitious."

---

[1] This translation is from Kaegi-Arrowsmith, *The Rig Veda,* p. 35. The immediately following translations are taken from the same work.

To the God of the destroying storm he prays:

> "Let me through thy best medicines, O Rudra,
> My life on earth prolong a hundred winters.
> From us dispel all hatred and oppression,
> On every side calamity drive from us.
>
> Where then, O Rudra, is thy hand of mercy,
> The hand that healing brings and softens sorrow,
> That takes away the ills which the gods send?
> Let me, O mighty one, feel thy forgiveness.
>
> The hero gladdened me amid tumult
> With greater might when I his aid entreated;
> Like some cool shade from the Sun's heat protected
> May I attain to Rudra's grace and refuge."

Again when he is penitent he would ask forgiveness of the god Varuna, the personification of the all-embracing heaven, and say:

> "If we to any dear and loved companion
> Have evil done, to brother or to neighbour,
> To our own countryman or to a stranger,
> That sin do thou O Varuna forgive us."

Or,

> "Forgive the wrongs, committed by our fathers,
> What we ourselves have sinned in mercy pardon;
> My own misdeeds do thou O God take from me,
> And for another's sin let me not suffer."

Or, again,

> "If ever we deceived like cheating players,
> If consciously we have erred or all unconscious
> According to our sin do not thou punish;
> Be thou the singer's guardian in thy wisdom."

But besides these prayers, we sometimes find poems

composed by the Vedic people, descriptive of their varied experiences of ordinary life. Thus a gambler gives his experience as follows:

"My wife has never angered me nor striven,
Was ever kind to me and my companions;
Though she was faithful to me, I have spurned her,
For love of dice, the only thing I value.

The gambler's wife deserted mourns; his mother
Laments her son, she knows not where he wanders.
And he in debt and trouble, seeking money,
Remains at night beneath the roof of strangers.

And when I say that I will play no longer,
My friends abandon me and all desert me;
Yet then again I hear the brown dice rattling
I hasten, like a wanton to her lover."

Again we read:

"The gambler hurries to the gaming table,
'Today I'll win,' he thinks in his excitement.
The dice inflame his greed, his hopes mount higher;
He leaves his winnings all with his opponent."

When we read these hymns we see in them the simple prayers of a simple primitive people impressed with the inexplicable and varied phenomena of a tropical climate. They turn to the forces behind the latter as personified deities, describing the phenomena and offering their simple prayers. We find in these prayers experiences of simple wonder, of sufferings and of simple enjoyments. But when we come to the sacrificial stage of development we find a religious outlook in which the independent simple meanings of the

hymns possess importance only for their sacrificial
utterance in particular contexts. During the particular
ritual observances the different verses were often torn
out of their contexts and were combined with others
which apparently had little or no relation with them
and no conceivable bearing on the performances during
which they were chanted or uttered. They were simply
the means for the performance of the sacrifices. Their
simple meanings as descriptions of things or events or
phenomena or ideas were dropped from consideration.
The value attached to them centered about their being
uttered or chanted in particular Vedic sacrifices in accordance with certain sacrificial canons of interpretation. The entire significance of these hymns consisted
either in their use as directions for the performance of
certain sacrificial duties or in their utterance in these
sacrifices under prescribed conditions as found in the
sacrificial manuals, the Brahmanas, which were considered as part of the Vedas. Thought and feeling
were driven from their places of importance in human
nature, and the whole emphasis was laid on the interpretation of the Vedic literature as a system of duties
involving commands and prohibitions, and nothing
else. Some of these duties were compulsory, while
others were voluntary in the sense that they had to be
performed only when one wanted to secure some desired end unattainable by any means discoverable by
his reason or experience.   8

The authority which this system of Vedic injunctions and prohibitions was supposed to possess was so
high as to demand the entire submission of one's will

and thought. Their claims did not stand in need of any justification by reason or logic, for they were supposed to be guides in a sphere where reason and experience were utterly helpless. The only fruitful way in which reason could be employed with regard to these Vedic commands was by accepting their authority and then trying to explain them in such a way that their mysterious nature might be reconciled to us. These Vedic commands cannot be described as "revelations" in the ordinary Christian sense of the term; for the latter presupposes the existence of a living God able and willing to bestow the body of truths that man requires, whereas the Vedic commands are devoid of any notion of a law-giver. This sacrificial mysticism, if it may be so called, does not recognize any God or supreme being from whom these commands emanate or who reveals them to man. The commands are taken as eternal truths, beginningless and immortal, revealing themselves to man and demanding man's submission to them. Nevertheless they are not spiritual or inner truths revealed from within man himself; they are external and impersonal commands which contain within themselves the inscrutable secrets of nature and of the happiness of man.   9

The fact that the Vedas were regarded as revelations of eternal truths, truths which no human reason could ever challenge, naturally divested reason of confidence in its ability to unravel the mysteries of man and of the world. Even in the somewhat later days of the evolution of Vedic culture, when there grew up a school of thinkers who disbelieved the claim that the whole of the Vedas were nothing but a body of commands and prohibitions and who held that there were at least some particular portions of the Vedas which dealt with the eternal truths of spiritual facts and experiences of reality, the belief remained unshaken that what the Vedas gave one as truths were unshakeable and unchallengeable by reason or by experience. This means a definite lowering or degradation of reason in its capacity as truth-finder. Reason calls for counter-reason and leads through an endless regressus without ever being able to lead to truth. The Vedas, then, are the only repository of the highest truths, and the function of reason is only to attempt to reconcile these truths with our experience and sense-observation. It is surprising that reason has continued to remain in this subordinate position throughout the development of Indian religious and philosophical thought almost to our own days. No change, no new idea could be considered to be right or could be believed by the people, unless it could also be shown that it had the sanction of the Vedas. Reason was never trusted as the only true and safe guide.   10

The word "mysticism" is a European word with a definite history. Most European writers have used it to denote an intuitive or ecstatic union with the deity, through contemplation, communion, or other mental experiences, or to denote the relationship and potential union of the human soul with ultimate reality. But I should for my present purposes like to give it a wider meaning which would include this and the other different types of mysticism that I may be discussing in the course of this series of lectures. I should like to define mysticism as a theory, doctrine, or view that considers reason to be incapable of discovering or of realising the nature of ultimate truth, whatever be the nature of this ultimate truth, but at the same time believes in the certitude of some other means of arriving at it. If this definition be accepted, then this ritualistic philosophy of the Vedas is the earliest form of mysticism that is known to India or to the world. This Vedic mysticism prepared the way for the rise of the other forms of mysticism that sprang up in India. Subsequent lectures will deal with these later forms, in some of which at least it will be easy to notice their similarity to Western types of mysticism with which Western readers are more or less familiar.   11

The main elements of the sacrificial mysticism of the Vedas may be summarised as follows: First, a belief that the sacrifices when performed with perfect accuracy, possess a secret, mysterious power to bring about or produce as their effect whatever we may desire either in this life or in the hereafter. Second, the conception of an unalterable law—involved in such invariable and unfailing occurrences of effects consequent upon the performance of these sacrifices. Third, an acceptance of the impersonal nature of the Vedic literature, as having existed by itself from beginningless time and as not created or composed by any person, human or divine. Fourth, the view that the Vedic literature embodies nothing but a system of duties involving commands and prohibitions. Fifth, a recognition of the supreme authority of the Vedas as the only source of the knowledge of ultimate truths which are far beyond the powers of human reason. Sixth, the view that truth or reality, whether it be of the nature of commands or of facts (as was maintained by the later Vedic schools of thought, the Upanishads), could be found once for all in the words of the Vedas. Seventh, the belief that the Vedic system of duties demands unfailing obedience and submission. Two definite characteristics emerge from these: first, the transcendent, mysterious, and secret power of the sacrifices, replacing the natural forces personified as gods; second, the ultimate superiority of the Vedas as the source of all truths, and as the unchallengeable dictators of our duties, leading to our material well-being and happiness. The assumption of the mysterious omnipotence of sacrifices, performed by following the authoritative injunctions of the Vedas independently of reason or logical and discursive thought, forms the chief trait of the mysticism of the Vedic type. There is nothing here of feeling or even of intellect, but a blind submission, not to a person but to an impersonal authority which holds within it an unalterable and inscrutable law, the secret of all powers which we may want to wield in our favor. 12

The next step in the development of this type of mysticism consists in the growth of a school of thought which sought to intellectualise the material sacrifices. It encouraged the belief that it was quite unnecessary actually to perform the sacrifices requiring the expenditure of enormous sums of money for the collection of materials and for labor. The same results

might be as well obtained through certain kinds of
meditation or reflection. Thus, instead of the actual
performance of a horse sacrifice, in which the immola-
tion of a horse is accompanied by other rituals engag-
ing the services of large numbers of men and the expenditure of funds such as kings alone could provide,
one might as well think of the dawn as the head of a
horse, the sun as its eye, the wind as its life, the heaven
as its back, the intervening space as its belly, the sky
as its flesh and the stars as its bones. Such a meditation, or rather concentrated imagining of the universe as a cosmic horse, would, it was maintained, produce all the beneficial results that could be expected
from the performance of an actual horse sacrifice.
Thus, these attempts to intellectualise sacrifices took
the form of replacing by meditation the actual sacrifices, and this substitution was believed to produce results which were equally beneficial. This meditation
by substitution gradually took various forms: certain
letters of the alphabet had, for example, to be thought
of, or meditated upon, as Brahman or some other deity,
or as vital functions of the body, or as some personified nature deity. This meditation was supposed to
produce beneficial results. It should not be supposed
that the sacrificial forms were entirely supplanted by
these new forms of substitution-meditations. Rather
did they spring up side by side with them. These forms
of meditation did not mean prolonged contemplation,
or any logical process of thinking, but merely the simple practice of continually thinking of one entity,
process, or letter as another entity or process.   13

Even in modern India there are still many men who believe that the repetition of mystical formulas (apparently meaningless combinations of letters, or the names of some deities) is capable of producing beneficial results. Even the worship of a round or an oval stone as the god Vishnu or Siva, or again the worship of a waterjug or an image as a particular god or goddess, is nothing but a modified form of substitution-meditation, one thing being considered and meditated upon as another. These practices are to be distinguished from the ordinary spells and incantations commonly believed in by uneducated people. These substitution-meditations are often believed to be productive of virtue. They form the normal modes of worship of the ordinary Hindu and have now taken the place of the old sacrifices. Nevertheless the old Vedic sacrifices are also to a certain extent performed on occasions of marriages and other domestic ceremonies, as an indispensable part of those ceremonies which still claim to belong entirely to the Vedic order. 14

But, refraining from further references to modern India, let us pick up our thread of discussion and note the next stage in the development of the substitution-meditations. Although the latter were in their conception doubtless as mystical and magical as the old sacrifices, they represent an advance. For in them the mystical powers are supposed to reside not in external performances, but in specific forms of meditation or thinking. This represents an approach toward a consciousness of self and toward a recognition of the mystical powers of thought and meditation of a peculiar type. But it was only after an almost endless and fruitless search that the highest idea of self and the highest idea of world mystery and its solution dawned in the minds of the Vedic thinkers. What we find at this stage is merely that the Vedic thinkers had become conscious of the activity of thought and of imagination, and had begun to realise that the activity involved in thinking ought to be considered to be as potent a power as the activity involved in the actual performances of material sacrifices. Man's inner thought and his performance of sacrificial duties in the world outside are both regarded as capable of producing mysterious changes and transformations in nature which would benefit man. Passages are to be found in the literature where the vital and other inner processes of the self are compared with a sacrifice. The three periods of human life are considered as being the same as the three bruisings of the sacrificial plant soma; and the functions of hungering, eating and begetting are considered to be the same as the different ceremonies of the soma sacrifice. Logical thinking in Vedic times seems to have taken the form of crude generalisation. The fundamental operation of logical thinking is generalisation based on a scrutiny of facts of experience, noting differences and avoiding false identifications. But in the early stages of Vedic thinking, generalisations were very crude and based on insufficient data, slurring points of difference and making bold identifications. Thus from the fact that we perspire through heat, there arose the cosmological belief that out of fire there came water. From observation of three principal colors, red, white and black (the colors of fire, water and earth) sprang the idea that the universe is made up of the three elements, viz., fire, water and earth. It was thought that wherever there was red, it was due to the existence of fire, wherever there was white it was due to the existence of water, and wherever there was black, it was due to the existence of earth.   15

By a similar loose process of generalisation the word Brahman came to denote the Vedic verses, truth, sacrifices, and knowledge. Etymologically the word means "The Great." Probably it signified vaguely and obscurely the mysterious power underlying these sacrifices and the substitution-meditations. Both the ideas involved in the conception of Brahman as the highest power and the highest knowledge were derived from the notion of the sacrifices. Thus we read in the celebrated man-hymn of the Rig Veda that the gods offered the supreme man as a sacrifice and that from this great oblation all living creatures, as well as the atmosphere, sky, earth and the four quarters, came into being. Three parts of this supreme man transcend the world while one part of him is the whole world about us; and yet, he is himself both the sacrifice and the object of the sacrifice.

But while I have just emphasised the importance of the mysticism of sacrifice in the development of the mystical conception of Brahman as the supreme being, it would be wrong to hold that the mysticism of the sacrifices is alone responsible for the evolution of the great concept of Brahman. Side by side with the concept found in the Rig Veda of the many gods as personifications of the forces of nature, there was also growing a tendency toward the conception of one supreme being, and this tendency gradually gained in force. Thus, in Rig Veda X. 114.5 we find a verse in which it is said that the deity is one, though he is called by various names. One of the hymns (R. V. X. 129), again, runs as follows:

"Then there was neither Aught nor Naught, no air nor sky
    beyond.
What covered all? Where rested all? In watery gulf pro-
    found?
Nor death was then, nor deathlessness, nor change of night
    and day.
That one breathed calmly, self-sustained; naught else beyond
    it lay.
Gloom hid in gloom existed first—one sea eluding view.
The one a void in chaos wrapt, by inward fervor grew.
Within it first arose desire, the primal germ of mind,
Which nothing with existence links, as ages searching find.
The kindling ray that shot across the dark and drear abyss,—
Was it beneath or high aloft? What bard can answer this?
There fecundating powers were found and mighty forces
    strove,—
A self-supporting mass beneath, and energy above.
Who knows and who ever told, from whence this vast crea-
    tion rose?
No gods had then been born. Who then can e'er the truth
    disclose
Whence sprang this world, whether framed by hand divine
    or no,—
Its lord in heaven alone can tell, if he can show."[2]

---

[2] The translation is taken from Muir's *Original Sanskrit Texts,* Vol. V.

Again, in the Atharva Veda (X, 7.) we find a hymn dedicated to Skambha where the different parts of this deity are identified not only with the different parts of the material world but also with a number of moral qualities such as faith, austere fervor, truthfulness, etc. All the thirty-three gods of the Vedas are contained within him and bow down to him. He is also called Brahman, "The Great." In the next hymn of the Atharva Veda (X. 8) Brahman is adored and spoken of as presiding over the past and the future, and he is said to be residing within our hearts and to be the self which never decays but is self-existent and self-satisfied. This appears to be very much like the idea of the Upanishads of which I shall speak in my next lecture. In the Shatapatha Brahmana, also, we hear of Brahman as having created the gods; and in the Taittiriya Brahmana, Brahman is said to have created the gods and the entire world.   17

Thus we find that the conception of one great being who created the world and the gods, and who is also the power presiding over our lives and spirits, was gradually dawning in the minds of a few people. And though the sacrificial theory tended to lead away from the ordinary meanings of these Vedic hymns, the development of the sacrificial theory itself also made for the conception of some mysterious force which reconciled the destinies of the world and nature with those of men and their desires. This mysterious power, it was held, is resident not only in things external but also in activities of the inner life; it manifests itself in the power of thought, as is exemplified by the mysterious efficacy of the substitution-meditations. What was the nature of this mysterious power? It is difficult to answer this question. We have seen that its conception varied in significance according to the mode of its development and the sources from which it evolved. But when once the conception was formed, all these constituent notions were mixed together. People regarded Brahman as the highest, but they did not know how Brahman was to be known. Those who started with the sacrificial bias, thought substitution-meditations to be the way to a knowledge of Brahman. And so we find various instructions regarding meditation upon objects, such as the wind, life, fire, etc., —even upon unmeaning letters. 18

But parallel with this tendency went another, viz., an intellectual search after Brahman, the highest, which displayed a contempt for sacrifices. We find Brahmins going out of their own sphere to warrior castes and kings for secret instruction about the nature of Brahman. There are narratives in which we find that kings belonging to the warrior caste fill proud Brahmins with a sense of discomfiture by exposing the ignorance of the latter concerning the secret nature of Brahman. Thus Balaki Gargya approached King Ajatashatru with the request to be allowed to explain to him the nature of Brahman. He then tried twelve times in succession to define Brahman as the presiding person in the sun, moon, lightning, ether, wind, fire, water, etc.; and in each case King Ajatashatru refuted him by showing the lower position that such presiding persons occupy in the whole of the universe, whereas

Brahman should be that which is the highest. Again, we find another narrative in which five Brahmins meet and discuss the question, "What is our Atman and what is Brahman?" They proceed to Uddalaka Aruni with the question. When Uddalaka mistrusts his ability to answer the question, all six go to King Ashvapati Kaikeya for instruction. King Ashvapati first asks them what it is that they worship as Atman or Brahman, anticipating their error that they still regard Atman or Brahman as a new kind of external divinity. The six Brahmins explain Atman in succession as the heaven, the sun, the wind, space, water, and the earth, and in so doing assume it to be an objective and an external deity more or less like the old Vedic deities. This shows us a stage of thought in which people somehow understood Brahman to be the highest principle, but yet found it difficult to shake off their old conceptions of external deities or personifications of nature. Again we find Sanatkumara instructing Narada regarding the nature of Brahman. In so doing Sanatkumara starts from "Name," by which he probably understands all conceptual knowledge. With his peculiar logic, which is difficult for us to follow, he observes that speech is greater than name, that mind is greater than speech, that imagination is greater than mind, and so on. Passing in succession through a number of such concepts, from lower to higher, he ultimately stops at that which is absolutely great, the unlimited, beyond which there is nothing and within which is comprehended all that is to be found in the outer and the inner world.   19

The most important point to be noted in the development of this stage of thought is that worship or prayer is possible only as directed toward a deity conceived with limited powers and as occupying a subordinate position in the universe. But with reference to that which is conceived as the highest truth and the highest power, there is no longer the possibility of external forms of worship. We shall find in the next lecture not only that it is not possible to worship Brahman but that it is not possible to reach Brahman by logical thought or any kind of conceptual apprehension. Thus in a Upanishadic story, referred to by Shankara, we are told of a person who approached a sage Bahva and sought from him instructions regarding the nature of Brahman. Bahva did not speak. He was asked a second time; still he did not speak. Yet again he was asked, but still he did not speak. When the inquirer became annoyed by this, Bahva told him that he was, from the first, by his silence telling him how Brahman was to be described: Brahman is silence and so cannot be represented in speech. There are, however, unmistakable indications that there were still some who believed that even the highest could be worshipped and adored and that men could still submit themselves to Him as to the highest personal God who comprehends us all and controls us all. But the idea that was gradually gaining ground with some of the most important sages, and which will be expounded in the next lecture, was that Brahman, as the highest, is no ordinary personal God who can be induced by worship to favor us or who can be approached by the pure intellect or even by feeling. Brahman still retains its mysterious character as the highest power, truth, being and bliss which can neither be worshipped nor known by ordinary means of knowledge. But its nature can be realised, and realised so perfectly that the realisation will be like the bursting of a shell of light, a revelation which will submerge the whole of one's life together with all that it contains. The next lecture will describe this type of mysticism of the Upanishads, which represents one of the highest and best, and undoubtedly one of the most distinctive, types of mysticism that India has produced. [20]

The Upanishads form the concluding portions of the Vedic literature, both chronologically from the point of view of the development of ideas. They were composed later than the priestly manuals, the Brahmanas, and the manuals of substitution-meditations in the Aranyaka literature, and they form the most authoritative background of all later Hindu philosophical thought. They possess the high authority of the Vedas and are the source of the highest wisdom and truth. The word "Upanishad" has been interpreted etymologically by Shankara to mean "that which destroys all ignorance and leads us to Brahman." It has also been interpreted to mean a secret or mystical doctrine, or a secret instruction, or a secret and confidential sitting. I have elsewhere, in my *History of Indian Philosophy,* shown how all the different systems of orthodox Indian philosophy look to the Upanishads for light and guidance, differently interpreting the Upanishad texts to suit their own specific systems of thought.

Eleven of these, Isha, Kena, Katha, Prashna, Mundaka, Mandukya, Taittiriya, Aitareya, Chandogya, Brihadaranyaka, and Svetashvatara, are probably the oldest. They vary greatly in length: while the Isha Upanishad would occupy but a single printed page, Brihadaranyaka would occupy at least fifty pages. Since the longer ones probably contain compositions of different periods and of different authorship they represent various stages of evolution and exhibit different intentions. Being the concluding portions of the Vedas, they are called the Vedanta. Their interpretations by different later writers gave rise to different systems of Vedanta philosophy. (One of these well-known forms of Vedanta philosophy was made known to the western world for the first time by a gifted Hindu, Svami Vivekananda.) The Upanishads themselves, however, do not seem to have been written in a systematic, well-connected and logical form. They are mystical experiences of the soul gushing forth from within us; they sparkle with the beams of a new light; they quench our thirst, born at their very sight. It was of these that the German philosopher Schopenhauer said: "How does every line display its firm and definite and throughout harmonious meaning. From every sentence deep, original, and sublime thoughts arise and the whole is pervaded by a high and holy and earnest spirit. . . . In the whole world there is no study, except that of the originals, so beneficial and so elevating as that of the Upanishads. It has been the solace of my life, it will be the solace of my death." Cases are known in which even Christian missionaries, sent out to India to teach church doctrines to clergymen or to preach Christianity among the Indians, became so fascinated by the high and lofty teachings of the Upanishads that they introduced the teaching of the Upanishads in the Church and as a consequence were compelled to resign their posts. To Hindus of all denominations there is nothing higher and holier than the inspired sayings of the Upanishads. To them we shall address our attention in the next lecture. **21**

LECTURE II
MYSTICISM OF THE UPANISHADS

LECTURE II

THE MYSTICISM OF THE UPANISHADS

IN the last lecture reference was made to a few of the monotheistic hymns of the Rig Veda and the Atharva Veda. Others might be cited; for instance, the adoration hymn to Hiranyagarbha (R. V. X. 121) who is therein described as the lord of the universe.

"In the beginning rose Hiranyagarbha,
Born as the only lord of all existence.
This earth he settled firm and heaven established:
What god shall we adore with our oblations?
Who gives us breath, who gives us strength, whose bidding
All creatures must obey, the bright gods even;
Whose shade is death, whose shadow life immortal:
What god shall we adore with our oblations?
Who by his might alone became the monarch
Of all that breathes, of all that wakes or slumbers,
Of all, both man and beast, the lord eternal:
What god shall we adore with our oblations?
Whose might and majesty these snowy mountains,
The ocean and the distant stream exhibit;
Whose arms extended are these spreading regions:
What god shall we adore with our oblations?
Who made the heavens bright, the earth enduring,
Who fixed the firmament, the heaven of heavens;
Who measured out the air's extended spaces:
What god shall we adore with our oblations?"[1]

---

[1] Translation taken from Kaegi-Arrowsmith, *The Rig Veda,* p. 88 f.

Or one may point to such hymns as the following:

> "Who is our father, our creator, maker,
> Who every place doth know and every creature,
> By whom alone to gods their names were given,
> To him all other creatures go to ask him."[2]

But such hymns are not numerous and probably belong to the last epoch of the composition of the Vedic hymns. Most of the Vedic hymns exhibit a conspicuous tendency toward the polytheistic personification of nature. From most of them the monotheistic tendency is well-nigh absent.   1

So, also, the literature of the sacrificial manuals, the Brahmanas, emphasizes the doctrine of the sacrifice. The adoration hymns of the different gods have lost their independent value and are esteemed only on account of the fact that these verses, sometimes mutilated and torn out of their context, are uttered or chanted in connection with various sacrificial rituals. This literature also contains some passages of a monotheistic or pantheistic character; but the emphasis is almost entirely on the performance of the sacrifices. In the Aranyaka literature, which contains the substitution-meditations, the value and power of thought is realized for the first time. But it is only in the Upanishads that one finds the earliest instances of a sincere and earnest quest after Brahman, the highest and the greatest.   2

The most important characteristic which distinguishes the science of Brahman from the science of the

---

[2] R. V. X. 82.3, as translated by Kaegi-Arrowsmith.

sacrifices consists in the fact that the former springs
entirely from inner, spiritual longings, while the latter
is based almost wholly on mundane desires. The science of sacrifice aimed at the acquirement of merit,
which could confer all the blessings of life in consequence of due obedience to the Vedic and ritualistic injunctions and prohibitions. The science of Brahman,
however, did not seek any ordinary blessings of life.
It proceeded from the spiritual needs of our soul which
could be satisfied only by attaining the highest aim.
All that is mortal, all that is transient and evanescent,
all that gives men the ordinary joys of life, such as
wealth or fame confer, are but brute pleasures and
brute satisfactions, which please only so long as men
allow themselves to be swayed by the demands of their
senses. In the hurry and bustle of our modern life,
of rapid movements over land, sea and air, in this age
of prolific scientific inventions and appliances which
add to our material comforts and luxury, in this age
of national jealousies and hatreds, which in the name
of patriotism and freedom often try to enslave others
or monopolize the necessities and luxuries of life for
the use of the people of a particular country, it is
easy to forget that we have any needs other than the
purely material ones. With all the boasted culture
of our modern age, with all our advancement of science and progress, do we ever stop to think just what
we mean by progress? We have no doubt discovered
many new facts of nature, and brought many natural
forces under our control. But like vultures soaring
high in the air, with greedy eyes fixed on the bones

and flesh of the carrion in the field below, are we not, in all our scientific soarings, often turning our greedy eyes to sense gratifications and trying to bind science to the attainment of new comforts and luxuries? The new comforts and luxuries soon become absolute necessities, and we eagerly press forward to the invention of some other new modes of sense gratification and luxury. Science debased to the end of spreading death and of enslaving humanity, or to the end of procuring newer and newer sensations, a life spent in the whirlpool of fleeting pleasures, varied, subtle, and new, and in the worship of the almighty dollar is what most of us tend to call progress. We live more for the body than for the soul. Our body is our soul; our body is our highest Brahman. The story is told in the Chandogya Upanishads that Virochana and Indra went to Prajapati to receive instructions regarding the nature of the self, or of Brahman the highest. Prajapati gave a course of false instructions, apparently to test the powers of discrimination of his two pupils Virochana and Indra. He asked them to get themselves well-dressed and appear at their best, and then to look into a mirror. When they did so and saw the image of their own bodies in the mirror, Prajapati told them that it was their well-dressed bodies reflected in the mirror that was the true self and the highest Brahman; and they went away satisfied with the answer. Indra, indeed, later returned to Prajapati dissatisfied with the answer; but Virochana (probably an old ancestor of ours) was satisfied with the answer that there is nothing higher than what appears to our senses, our earthly body, and our earthly joys.   3

But what a different answer do we get from Maitreyi, the wife of Yajnavalkya in the Brihadaranyaka Upanishad II. 4. Yajnavalkya, wishing to become a hermit, explained to his two wives Maitreyi and Katyayani that he wished to divide his wealth between them so that they might live independently while he was away seeking his higher spiritual destiny. But Maitreyi replied: "Well, sir, if you could give me all the wealth of the world, could I become immortal by that?" "No," said Yajnavalkya, "you will only live in pleasure as the rich men do, but I can promise you no hope of immortality through wealth." Maitreyi replied, "Well, sir, what shall I do with that with which I cannot be immortal? Tell me if you know anything by which I may be immortal."   4

It is this spiritual craving for immortality that distinguishes the mental outlook of the sages of the Upanishads from our own. Yet this desire for immortality is no mere desire for personal survival continuing the enjoyment of pleasures under newer and happier conditions of life, whether in this world or in heaven. This quest for immortality, as it is found in the Upanishads, is in no sense a yearning for personal immortality, the decayless, diseaseless, deathless existence of the individual with his body in full vigor of youth. Neither is it the desire for a bodiless existence of a self fond of sensual joys and sense gratifications and fettered by all the needs and necessities of mundane relations and mundane gratifications. This quest for immortality is identical with the quest of the highest self, the highest truth and reality, the highest Brahman. It is the perception and realization of the inner spring of our life and the inmost spirituality of man as he is within himself, beyond the range of sense and of discursive thought. If it were a sense-feeling —color, taste, touch, or sound—it might easily be pointed out as this or that sense-datum. It is an ineffable, non-conceptual, inner experience, lying in its own unfathomable depth. When a lump of salt is thrown into the sea, it is entirely dissolved in it; by no means can any part of the lump be recovered in its original form, but every part of the water tastes saline. Similarly, when this stage of supra-consciousness (*prajnana*) is reached, all ordinary experiences are submerged and dissolved in this great, infinite, limitless, homogeneous experience. Like the calm and changeless consciousness of deep, dreamless sleep, is this stage where all duality has vanished: there is no person who knows, nor anything that he is aware of. Ordinary knowledge presupposes a difference between ourselves, our knowledge, and that of which we are aware. When I see a color, there is the "I" which sees, there is the knowledge of the color and also the color itself. When I smell, there is the "I" that smells and the smell; when I think, there is the "I" that thinks and that which is thought; when I speak there is the "I" that speaks and that which is spoken. No one would for a moment think of identifying these. But at this stage of the non-conceptual intuition of the self —an unspeakable, ineffable experience—there is no

trace of any duality, and we have one whole of blissful experience wherein is distinguished no one that
knows and nothing that he is aware of. All ordinary
states of knowledge imply a duality of knower and
that which is known; but this is an experience where
all duality has vanished.   5

Nevertheless this experience is not something which
is wholly beyond, or wholly out of all relation with,
our conscious states of dual experience. For it is the
basis, or background, as it were, of all our ordinary
knowledge involving the knower and the known. In
music, the different notes and tones cannot be grasped
separately from and independently of the music itself,
and when we are busy in apprehending separately the
different notes we miss the music or the harmony
which is in itself a whole of experience 'that cannot be
taken in parts, in the multiplicity of the varied notes.
So it is with this ineffable experience, which in reality
underlies all our ordinary experiences and states of
knowledge as the basis or ground of them all; when we
are lost in the discursive multiplicity of our ordinary
experience, we miss this underlying reality. But when
once again we are in touch with it, our so-called personality is as it were dissolved in it, and there ensues
that infinitude of blissful experience in which all distinctions are lost. Whatever is dear to me, as e. g.,
father, mother, wife, money, fame, etc., is so because I
love my own self so dearly. It is because I can find
the needs of my self best realized through these that
I love these. None of these can be ends in themselves;
it is only the self that can be an end unto itself, ir-

respective of any other ulterior end or motive. None
of the many-sided interests, desires, and activities of
the self represent the self in its entirety or in its essence. It is only this supra-conscious experience,
which actually underlies them all, that can be called the
real self and that for which everything else exists.
Everything else is dear to me because my self is dear
to me; but this supra-conscious experience underlies
the so-called personality, or self, as its very essence,
truth and final reality.   6

It is indeed difficult for us, with the traditions and
associations of our modern world, to believe in the
reality of this intuitional experience, unless we attempt
to realize it ourselves—unless, by turning our minds
entirely away from sense-objects and sense-enjoyments, we deliberately, with faith and firmness,
plunge into the depths of this new kind of experience.
It cannot be expressed in words or understood by conceptual thought; it reveals itself only to supra-conscious experience. The language of the sages of the
Upanishads seems strange to us; but we cannot hope
to understand a thing of which we have had no experience. Talk to a child of ten about the romantic
raptures of love felt by a pair of lovers, or of the
maddening intoxication of sense cravings; what would
he understand of it? Talk to a Greenlander about the
abominable heat of an African desert; will he be able
to imagine it? When an experience is to be realized,
the powers of mere logical thinking or of abstraction
or of constructive imagination are not sufficient for the
purpose. Only another realization of the same experi-

ence can testify to its truth. We are here concerned
with an experience which is non-conceptual, intuitive,
and ultimate. But, what is more, subtle, fine and
formless as it is, it is said to be the source, basis, and
ground of everything else. According to a story told in
the Chandogya Upanishad VI, when Shvetaketu returned after a stay of twelve years at the house of his
preceptor, where he studied all the Vedas, he became
arrogant, considered himself to be a wise man, and
hardly ever talked with others. His father said to
him: "Well, Shvetaketu, what have you learned that
you seem to think yourself so wise? Do you know
that which when once known everything else becomes
known? When you once know what iron is, you
know all that can be made out of iron, for these are
in essence nothing but iron; we can distinguish the
iron vessels from iron only by their specific forms and
names. But whatever may be their names and forms,
the true essence in them all, whether they be needles,
pans or handles, is nothing but iron. It is only that
you find therein so many forms and names. What are
these names and forms worth without the essence? It
is the essence, the iron, that manifests itself in so
many forms and names; when this iron is known, all
that is made of iron is also known. It is the ineffable
reality, the ultimate being which is the essence of
everything else. As rivers which flow into the sea
lose all their individuality in it and cannot be distinguished, so all divergent things lose their individuality
and distinctness when they are merged in this highest
being, the ultimate reality from which they have all

sprung forth. Fine and subtle though this experience be, yet it is in reality the entire universe of our knowledge. A small seed of an oak tree when split open reveals nothing that we can call worth noting, yet it is this fine kernel of the seed that holds within it the big oak tree." 7

The chief features of this Upanishad mysticism are the earnest and sincere quest for this spiritual illumination, the rapturous delight and force that characterize the utterances of the sages when they speak of the realization of this ineffable experience, the ultimate and the absolute truth and reality, and the immortality of all mortal things. Yet this quest is not the quest of the God of the theists. This highest reality is no individual person separate from us, or one whom we try to please, or whose laws and commands we obey, or to whose will we submit with reverence and devotion. It is, rather, a totality of partless, simple and undifferentiated experience which is the root of all our ordinary knowledge and experience and which is at once the ultimate essence of our self and the highest principle of the universe, the Brahman or the Atman. There is, indeed, another current of thought, evident in several passages of different Upanishads, in which Brahman is conceived and described as the theistic God. This will be dealt with separately later on. The special characteristic of the line of thought that has now been described is a belief in a superior principle which enlivens our life, thoughts, actions, desires and feelings, which is the inmost heart of the self of man, the immortal and undying reality unaffected by disease and death, and which is also the ultimate and absolute reality of the universe.   8

A story is told in the Katha Upanishad according to which King Vajashravasa made a sacrifice involving a gift of all the valuables that he possessed. When everything of the sort had been given away, he made a supplementary gift of his cows which were all old and useless. His son Naciketas, finding that these gifts would be more embarassing than useful to the recipient, disapproved of his father's action. He thought that his father had not finished giving his "all" until he, his son, was also given away. So he asked his father, "To whom are you going to give me?" He was dear to his father; so his father did not like this question and remained silent. But when the question was again and again repeated, the father lost his temper and said, "I give you over to death." Then Naciketas went to the place of Yama, the king of death, where he remained fasting for three days and nights. Yama, willing to appease him, requested him to take any boons that pleased him. Naciketas replied that men do not know what happens to people when they have passed from earthly life, whether they still continue to exist or whether they cease to exist; and he requested Yama to answer this question on which there were so many divergent opinions. Yama in answer said that this was a very difficult question and that even the gods did not know what becomes of man after he passes away from his earthly life; that, therefore, he would rather give Naciketas long life, big estates, gold in abundance, horses, elephants, and whatever else in the way of earthly enjoyment might seem to him desirable. But the philosophical quest was dearer to Naciketas than all the earthly goods that the king of death could bestow upon him. Money, he thought, can not satisfy man; money is of use only so long as a man lives, and he can live only so long as death does not take him away. This quest of the ultimate destiny of man, of his immortal essence, is itself the best and the highest end that our hearts may pursue. So Naciketas preferred to solve this mystery and riddle of life rather than to obtain all the riches of the world and all the comforts that they could purchase. 9

The king of death appreciated the wisdom of Naciketas' choice. He explained that there are two paths, the path of the good and the path of the pleasant, and that they are different paths, leading to two entirely different goals. The mad hankering after riches can only justify itself by binding us with ties of attachment to sense-pleasures which are short-lived and transitory. It is only the spiritual longing of man after the realization of his highest, inmost, truest, and most immortal essence that is good in itself, though it does not appeal to greedy people who are always hankering after money. Desire for money blinds our eyes, and we fail to see that there is anything higher than the desire for riches, or that there is anything intrinsically superior to our ordinary mundane life of sense-pleasures and sense-enjoyments. The nature of the higher sphere of life and of the higher spiritual experiences cannot be grasped by minds which are always revolving in the whirlpool of mad desires for riches and sense-enjoyments. As the sage, in his serene enjoyment of spiritual experiences, may well think sense-pleasures dull, insipid, and valueless, so the multitude who live a worldly life of ordinary pleasures and enjoyments, fail to perceive the existence of this superior plane of life and the demands of the spirit for the realization of its immortal essence. They think that nothing exists higher and greater than this mundane life of ordinary logical thought and sense-enjoyments. Most men live on this ordinary level of life; they see, hear, taste, touch and smell. They think and they argue. They have a mind which thinks, feels, and wills, and they have senses which seek their own gratification. They employ the former in the service of the latter and every day discover newer and subtler ways of sense-gratification; they also employ the latter to serve the former by furnishing sense data to guide and check the course of logical thought and the development of science. The more men, upon comparing opinions, find themselves agreeing that they possess nothing of a more lofty character, the more they cease to believe in the validity and truth of the existence of anything undying in man. They fail to notice that the life they are living has had the effect of chilling and freezing the clear flowing stream of spiritual experiences and of stifling the spiritual instincts and longings of the soul. Generations of lives spent without once turning the eyes to the spiritual light within have served to build up traditions, beliefs, and tendencies of such an order that faith in the existence

of the higher spirituality of man is lost. Discourse
about the spirituality of man in its highest sense appears to most men to be no more than a myth of by-
gone days or the result of the undue nervous excitation
or heated imagination of a religious intoxication. The
net result of our modern education, civilization, and
culture has been the disappearance of the belief that
there is anything higher than the gratification of man's
primitive instincts under such checks as society requires, the pursuit of the physical sciences, and the
successful employment of the art of reasoning for the
satisfaction of all the diverse interests of human beings. So Yama, the king of death, says to Naciketas
that the majority of the people do not believe that there
is anything higher than the ordinary mundane life, being content with the common concerns and interests of
life; that it is only the few who feel this higher call
and are happy to respond to it and to pursue a course
of life far above the reach of the common man.   10

But what is this undying spiritual essence, or existence? Cannot our powers of reasoning, as they are
employed in philosophical discussion or logical arguments, discover it? If they can, then at its best it can
be nothing loftier than thought and can not be considered as the highest principle by which even thought itself and all conscious processes, as well as the functioning of all sense-operations, are enlivened and vitalized. So Yama tells Naciketas that this highest spiritual essence in us cannot be known by discursive reason. Only persons who have realized this truth can
point this out to us as an experience which is at once

self-illuminating and blissful and which is entirely different from all else that is known to us. Once it is thus exhibited, those who have the highest moral elevation and disinclination to worldly enjoyments can grasp it by an inner intuitive contact with the reality itself (*adhyatmayoga*). This truth is indeed the culmination of all the teaching of the Vedas. 11

To Naciketas' question as to what becomes of men when they leave this earthly life, Yama's answer is that no one is ever born and no one ever dies. Birth and death pertain only to our physical bodies, but our essence is never born and never dies. The birth and death of the physical body may well be explained by reference to physical causes, and there is not much of a mystery therein. But man cannot be identified with his body, nor can he be identified simply with the life which he has in common with all other animals, and even with plants. Life, in a large measure, seems to be nothing but a harmonious functioning of the inner organs of the body; but no one would say that these movements of the organs can be called "man." There is a superior principle which vitalises and quickens the process of life, enlivens the activity of thought, moves the senses to their normal and regular operations, which is realized, or intuited, as the very essence of our inner illumination, and which is also the highest and ultimate principle underlying all things. 12

We are here face to face with the real mysticism of the Upanishads. This highest essence of man, the self, the Brahman, is difficult of perception; it is hidden, as in a deep cavern, in that deathless being who exists

from the beginning of all time and beyond all time. It
is the subtlest, the smallest of the small and yet the
greatest of the great. It exists changeless and just the
same one when everything else that it has vitalized has
ceased to exist. This, our inmost self, cannot be known
by much learning or scholarship, nor by sharp intelligence, nor by strong memory. It can only be known,
or intuited, by the person to whom it reveals its own
nature. In one place we are told that it can be intuited only by an inner, direct, and immediate touch.
In another place it is said that it can only be perceived
by those who have practised the perceiving of fine
truths by a superfine intelligence of the highest order
(Katha I. 3.12). The path to this superior intuition
is like the edge of a sharp razor, dangerous and difficult. It is beyond all sense-knowledge; and he who
intuits this secret truth of the beginningless, endless,
unchangeable and eternal overcomes all death. For,
once one realizes oneself to be identical with this highest principle, death and the fear of it sink into insignificant, illusory nothingness.   13

There is, however, another line of thought running
through the different Upanishads in which Brahman
appears as the supreme Lord from whom everything
has proceeded and who is the source of all energy.
Thus in the Kena Upanishad we find the query: "By
whose will and directed by whom does the mind work,
and directed by whom did life first begin? By whose
will does the organ of speech work, and led by whom
do the eye and the ear perform their respective functions?" Then comes the answer: "It is from Him

that the organ of speech, the ear, the eye, the mind and life have all derived their powers; He is the thought of thought, the mind of mind, and the life of life. So neither mind nor eye, neither ear nor speech, can tell us anything about Him, because neither the eye nor the ear nor the mind can reach Him, but He alone is the agent operative through all these organs and making the eye perceiver, the ear hearer, the mind a thinker and the life a living force. But He, in his own nature, cannot be grasped by any one of these." 14

A story is told to illustrate the greatness of Brahman as the supreme and all-powerful Lord. All the gods were at one time congratulating themselves on their own greatness, though all the while it was Brahman alone who was great. Brahman saw the false conceit of the gods and appeared before them as the all-powerful Lord. The gods sent the god of fire to him to enquire who this great Lord was. Agni, the god of fire, approached him and this great Lord asked Agni who he was and what he could do? Agni replied that he was the god of fire and could burn the whole world. Brahman then put before him a straw and asked him if he could burn it. Agni tried with all his might to burn it, but failed. Thereupon Agni returned to the gods saying that he could not learn who this great lord was. Vayu, the wind-god, approached Brahman and said that he was the wind-god and could blow away the whole world. Again Brahman placed a straw before him, asking him to blow it away if he could. Vayu also failed and came back to the other gods. Then Indra came forward to inquire who this great Lord was, but Brahman had already disappeared from the scene. Thereupon a bright glorious goddess appeared in the sky and told him that this supreme Lord was Brahman, that He alone was great, and that all the powers of the gods of fire, wind, etc., were derived from him.   15

It is said in the Katha VI. 1-3 that all the worlds are maintained in him. He is like a big tree which has its roots far below and its branches above, forming the visible universe around us. He is the great Life from which everything else has come into being. Nothing dare ignore, disobey, or outstrip Him. He is like a great thunder of fear over us all. It is by His fear that the fire and the sun give heat, that the wind blows, and that Death runs about. He is elsewhere described (Brrh. IV. IV. 22) as the controller, Lord and master of all. He is the Lord of all that has been and all that will be. He is the creator of the universe and the world belongs to Him and He to the world (Brrh. IV. IV. 13). Yet He is the inmost self of all living beings (*sarvabhutantaratma*) and the immortal inner controller of them all (*antaryamin*). But, though He is the controller and creator of all, yet it is He who has become this visible universe of diverse names and forms. Just as the wind and the fire appear in different forms, so He also appears in all the varied forms that present themselves to us in this world. Being one in Himself, He has become the visible many of the universe. But yet He is absolutely untouched by faults and defects of this mortal world. As the Sun which by its light illumines all colors and forms for the eye and is yet unaffected by the defects of our eyes, so the Brahman, who by his light has brought all things into existence and continues as their inmost essence, is yet wholly unaffected by their defects, their mortal and transitory forms. 16

Whether the teaching of the Upanishads is to be called pantheism or not will depend on the definition of pantheism. Certainly there are some passages such as those just considered which describe Brahman as having spread Himself in diverse forms in all the objects that we see around us. This might readily be taken as indication of some form of materialistic pantheism. But this is merely one phase or aspect of the matter. It seems to be contradicted by the idea of Brahman as the creator, ruler, and controller, by whose will everything moves and the order of events is kept in its right place undisturbed. Neither life nor death nor any of the powers of nature can transgress his orders; He is a thundering fear over us all, and yet He is also the bridge by which all the diverse things of the world are connected with one another and with man, their spiritual master. This latter conception, which is present in many passages of the Upanishads, is apparently dualistic and implies a personal God. The Shvetashvatara Upanishad abounds in passages of an avowedly dualistic character. There it is said that He alone is the Lord of all bipeds and quadrupeds, the protector and master of the universe, and yet is hidden in all beings. The duality between the individual soul and God is also definitely expressed in at least two of the earlier Upanishads, Mundaka 3. 1. 1 and Shvetashvatara 4. 6,

where, with reference to Brahman and the individual,
it is said that two birds which are alike in nature and
friendly to each other reside in the same tree, but that
one of them (the individual) eats sweet fruits (i. e.
of his own deeds) while the other is happy in
itself without eating any fruit whatsoever. In the
same Shvetashvatara Upanishad, the sage is described
as saying: "I know this great person who resides beyond all darkness (of sin and ignorance), as bright as
the sun. He who knows Him escapes death and there
is no other way of escape. There is nothing superior
to Him, and there is nothing which is greater than
Him, and there is nothing smaller than Him. He
stands alone by Himself in the Heavens unmoved like
a tree, and yet the world is filled by this person."
But this also is a passing phase. In a passage immediately preceding that in the Mundaka Upanishad
just referred to, it is said that Brahman is right before
us in the front; Brahman is behind us in the back;
Brahman is on the right and on the left. Again it is
said in the Katha Upanishad: "He who perceives
diversity in this world suffers the death of all deaths."
"He is the controller and the self of all beings; He
makes the one form many, being one He satisfies the
desires of the many."   17

The most important emphasis of the Upanishads
seems to be on that ineffable experience which lies
hidden in the background of all our experiences and
at the same time enlivens them all. Yet the experi-
encer himself is lost, and dissolved as it were, in this
superior experience, where there is neither experi-

encer nor that which is experienced. This experience, or state, cannot be intellectually grasped; it can only be pointed out as different from all that is known, or from all that can be described as "this" or "that." One can only assert that "It is not this," "It is not this." It is like the state of a deep dreamless sleep, like the feeling of intense bliss where neither the knower nor the known can be distinctly felt but where there is only the infinitude of blissful experience.   18

The various commentators upon the Upanishads belonging to different schools of thought and yet each interested to secure for himself the support of the Upanishads, have been fighting with one another for the last twelve hundred years or more to prove that the Upanishads are exclusively in favor of one party as against the others. Thus some contend that the Upanishads teach that Brahman alone exists and all the rest that appears is false and illusory. Others hold that the Upanishads favor the doctrine of modified duality of man in God and of God in man. Still others maintain that the Upanishads give us exclusively a doctrine of uncompromising duality. And so forth. Passages have often been twisted and perverted, and many new connections and contexts have been introduced or imposed upon the texts, to suit the fancy or the creed of the individual commentator. I think all these interpretations are biassed and onesided, and therefore inexact. The Upanishads reveal to us different phases of thought and experience, not a consistent dogmatic philosophy. The apparent inconsistency of the different phases of thought is removed if we take a psychological point of view and consider them as different stages of development in the experience of minds seeking to grasp a sublime, ultimate but inexpressible truth. This truth has a logic of its own, different from the logic of discursive thought wherein distinctions are firm and rigid, where concepts are like pieces of brick mortared together by the logical movement of thought. Its logic is that of experience in which the apparently contradictory ideas or thoughts lose their contradictoriness and become parts of one solid whole. The different phases of experience are lived through and enjoyed as inalienable parts of one great experience. When attempts are made to describe any particular phase of this experience it will naturally seem to conflict with the other phases in the eyes of those who have not the capacity of realising the concrete whole experience and who can only look at the phases from an external and a purely intellectual point of view where distinctions cannot be obliterated. When a lover embraces his beloved in his first kiss, he may feel her as the holiest angel, as his own dear life or as the embodiment of all his happiness, as, Shelley says, his "Spouse, Sister Angel, Pilot of the Fate,"

> "Of unentangled intermixture, made
>   By love, of light and motion; one intense
>   Diffusion, one serene Omnipresence."

But these epithets when applied to a woman can hardly be justified, according to intellectual standards, as properly applied, though the lover may have felt an indescribable sweetness of love in which all these diverse sentiments melted together to form its taste and flavor. The different phases of experience and belief which we find in the Upanishads need not therefore be taken out and pitted against one another. They may all be regarded as stages of experience between which the minds of the sages oscillated in attempting the realisation of a truth which was beyond speech, beyond thought and beyond all sense-perception. It was sometimes felt as the great over-lord, the controller, creator, ordainer, and master of all, sometimes as the blissful spiritual experience, and sometimes as the simple unity in which all duality has vanished.   19

This truth, person, or absolute—whatever it may be called—was felt as the highest embodiment of moral perfection. It is complete self-illumination, bodiless, faultless, sinless and pure. It is, as it were, covered by a cup of gold in such wise that we, looking at the shiny cup, miss the real treasure that lies concealed beneath. Its illumination reveals itself only when our minds have turned away from all the external lights of the outside world; for where this light is shining, all the other lights of the sun, the moon, and the stars have ceased to give light. The Upanishads tell us again and again that it cannot be perceived by any of our senses and that it cannot be comprehended by reasoning, or by logical and discursive thought, or by discussions, scholarship and much learning, or even by the reading of the scriptures. Only those who have ceased from all sinful actions and have controlled all their sense desires, who are unruffled by passions of all kinds and are at peace with themselves, can have the realization of this great truth by the higher intuitive knowledge (*prajnana,* as distinguished from *jnana,* or cognition). In Mundaka III.1, it is said that we can attain this self by truth, control, spiritual fervor and absolute extinction of all sex desires. Only the sages who have purged themselves of all moral defects and faults are capable of perceiving this holy spiritual light within themselves. The Upanishads never tire of repeating that the revelation of this truth is possible only through the most perfect moral purity which results in a natural illumination of intuitive perception when one seeks to attain this partless essence through meditation. Not only can this truth not be perceived by the eye or described in speech; but it cannot even be gained as a boon, or gift, by pleasing the gods or by ascetic practices or by sacrificial performances. It can only be attained by an intuition (*para*) which is superior in kind to the Vedic knowledge of sacrifices, called the lower knowledge (*apara*). By supreme moral elevation and untiring and patient search one can come in touch with Brahman and can enter into Him, but one must abandon all his mundane desires by which he is bound to earthly things. And when through this high moral elevation, control of desires, meditation and the like, one comes face to face with this highest reality, or Brahman, he is lost in it like rivers in the sea; nothing remains of him which he can feel as a separate individual, but he becomes one with Brahman. This is known by the seer through his heart when his senses have ceased to move and when his thought and intellect have come to a dead halt.   No one can describe what that existence is; one can only say that it is "being," nothing more.   Here all the knots of the heart are untied, all doubts are dispelled, and there is one spiritual light of unity that shines forth in its serene oneness.   20

LECTURE III
YOGA MYSTICISM

LECTURE III

YOGA MYSTICISM

THE last lecture dealt with the ineffable intuitive experience which the sages of the Upanishads regarded as absolute and ultimate in nature. The Upanishads, however, indicate no definite method for arriving at the perception of this truth. It is made clear that the pathway consists not in erudition or scholarship, and that it is not traversed by any sharpness of intelligence. The truth is such that it cannot be conceived by the human mind or described by language. One of the fundamental conditions of attaining it is the complete elevation of the moral life, including the absolute control of all passions and desires, the abandonment of worldly ambitions and hopes, and the attainment of an unruffled peace of mind. But the dawning of the supra-consciousness which can reveal this truth does not, even so, depend entirely on our own efforts; there is something like divine mercy that must be awaited. This self can only be realized by those to whom it reveals itself. The perfecting of our moral life is a prerequisite; but no method deliberately and consciously pursued is sufficient to bring us all the way into the full realization of the highest truth. In at least one or two of the Upanishads indications of a

different line of thought and method of realization
are to be found. Thus in Katha III, our senses are
compared with horses which are always running after
their respective sense-objects. He who is not wise
but is without control over his own mind cannot
control his senses, just as a bad driver cannot control
his horses. If anyone wishes to make his way to his
highest goal, he should have wisdom for his driver and
his mind as the reins of the horses of the senses. In
Katha VI, it is said that there is a state in which
the five senses, thought, intellect, and mind all cease to
operate, and this highest stage of absolute sense-re-
straint is called "Yoga," or spiritual union.   1

There are ample literary evidences that from very
early times—from at least 700 or 800 B. C.—people
were in the habit of concentrating their minds on particular objects and thereby stopping the movement of
the mind and the senses and achieving wonderful,
miraculous powers. It is difficult to say how the ancient Indians discovered this mode of mental control.
But it seems very probable that as at first practised
it did not form a part of any metaphysical system of
thought but was simply the practise of mental concentration and breath control for the sake of the re-
sulting peace and quietness of mind, as well as of the
miraculous powers which could be achieved thereby.
The powers of hypnotism, or mesmerism, seem to have
been very well known in ancient India and were also
included among the powers that could be derived from
the yoga practices.   2

A story is told in the Mahabharata (13.40) that

Devasharma, a sage, had a very beautiful wife, named Ruci, whom he carefully guarded from the seductive influences of Indra who desired to possess her. Once he had to go away to perform sacrifices at a distant place, and he left his wife under the protection of his pupil Vipula. The pupil knew that Indra could resort to many clever disguises and that it would be difficult to protect Ruci from him by guarding her by any external means. So he decided to enter into her mind by his powers of yoga and to control her behavior and speech from within. Accordingly, he sat in front of his teacher's wife and remained staring at her eyes, inhibiting all movements of his own body. In this way he entered into her body and remained there awaiting his teacher's return. Now Indra, thinking that the lady was alone in the house, came there in his fine and radiant form. He saw there the inanimate body of Vipula, the pupil, with its eyes absolutely motionless as if they were painted on canvas. He also saw the lady sitting there in all her resplendent beauty. On beholding Indra, she wished to rise and greet him; but being controlled from within by her husband's pupil, she could not succeed in doing as she desired. Indra spoke to her in his own charming manner, telling her that he had come there for her and that he was Indra. Perceiving that the lady was showing signs of becoming fascinated, Vipula controlled all her senses and limbs from within in such a way that, though she desired very much by rising from her seat to receive Indra, she could not do so. When Indra found her silent and unresponsive, he again spoke to her and

asked her to rise and receive him. Again, though she
wanted to welcome him, Vipula controlled her speech
so that she told Indra that he had no business to come
to her, and she was ashamed that she so spoke against
her will. Indra then understood the whole affair and
was much afraid. Vipula then returned to his own
body and took Indra to task for his misbehavior.   3

Many other stories, illustrating the various kinds of
miraculous powers of yoga, might be repeated. But
let us turn to a consideration of the principal use of
the yoga practices for the spiritual enlightenment, the
ultimate and absolute freedom of man, as described
by Patanjali, the great yoga writer of about 150 B. C.
Patanjali not only describes the principal yoga practices,
but he gives a philosophical basis to the whole system
and indicates, for the first time, how yoga may be
utilized for the emancipation of man from the bondage
of his mind and senses. It was explained in the last
lecture that the sages of the Upanishads believed in a
supra-conscious experience of pure self-illumination as
the ultimate principle, superior to and higher than any
of our mental states of cognition, willing, or feeling.
The nature of this principle is itself extremely mystical; many persons, no doubt, are unable to grasp its
character. It has been shown that, even in the days of
the Upanishads, it was recognized to be obscure, and
that the sages were never tired of saying that it could
neither be perceived by the eye nor conceived in
thought; but that, nevertheless, the sages believed in its
existence as the ultimate being and not as an experience of ecstatic feeling or any other kind of transient

psychological state. It was regarded as the real self and the ultimate reality. It is this view of self that is the root, as it were, of Indian mysticism.   4

If we ask ourselves what we understand by "I," we shall all find that, though it is in the most constant use, it is also the obscurest word in all our dictionaries. About the meaning of the word, in one sense we can never doubt; for there is no person who can ever doubt whether he is himself or another person. But when we try to understand what it definitely and actually means, it appears to be one of the most elusive of words. It certainly cannot designate merely our bodies; nor does it mean any particular idea or feeling of a temporary character. So we have to admit that while we all understand what it means we cannot define it. This is not the place to enter into all the recondite philosophical discussions to which the problem of the nature of the self has given rise. But some attempt must be made to explain what the Indians understood by the immortal and unchangeable self. Some believed this self to be the same in all persons, while others believed it to be many; but the conception of its nature was more or less the same in most of the systems of Indian thought. It was pure, contentless consciousness, altogether different from what we understand by idea, knowledge, or thought. Our thoughts and feelings are changeful; but this mysterious light of pure consciousness was changeless. The ultimate aim of the yoga processes (as of most of the Indian systems of thought) is to dissociate ourselves from our sensations, thoughts, ideas, feelings, etc., to learn that these are extraneous associations, foreign to the nature of self but adhering to it almost so inseparably that the true self cannot be easily discovered as a separate and independent entity.   5

But with the Indian sages this doctrine of a transcendent self was not merely a matter of speculative philosophy. For philosophy came to them much later than the actual practice of the liberation of this true self from the bondage of the association with all our so-called psychical states, ideas, feelings, emotions, images and concepts. It is very difficult for a Western mind of today to understand, or appreciate, the minds of the Indian seers. They felt a call from within the deep caverns of their selves—a call which must have started from a foretaste of their own true essence— which made all earthly pleasures or hopes of heavenly pleasures absolutely distasteful to them. They could feel satisfied only if they could attain this true freedom, their true self. To appreciate their experience at all one must, in imagination, take a long jump backward of about twenty-five centuries and across the waters of the Atlantic and the Indian oceans, and picture to oneself the valley of the lofty snow-capped peaks of the Himalayas looking high up to the infinite of the heavens and, far beyond, the peaceful groves and cottages where the innocence and forbearance of man had endeared him to trees and beasts alike, where no other sounds disturbed the serene forest-dwellers than the breezy rustling of the lofty Sal trees and the grovy palms. The necessities of the men who dwelt there were few. They often wore clothes made from birch bark, and ate fruits and vegetables that grew wild in the hermitage and rice which grew without much trouble of cultivation. The cows of the hermitage supplied them with milk and butter. They did not take any animal life for food; the birds ate from their hands, the soft-eyed gazelles roamed about their huts, made of straw or leaves of trees, and the peacocks danced in the shady groves of their forest walks. The clear, transparent waters of the holy river Ganges and other rivers watered their hermitages, and the cool breezes delightfully refreshed their bodies and minds when the wearisome tropical heat had relaxed their nerves and muscles into inaction. These men had no riches, and they did not seek them. Their natural needs were few, and it never occurred to them that these could be augmented or multiplied. They thought, rather, that what needs they had were in themselves too numerous and could be indefinitely curtailed. Even in rather recent times a story is told to the effect that a scholar in Bengal, called Ramnath, was visited by Raja Krishnachandra of Bengal who wanted to bestow riches on him and asked him if he had any wants. The scholar replied that he had plenty of rice in his house and that he could make his soup out of the sour leaves of the tamarind tree which grew in his yard; the only difficulty that he had was with regard to some intellectual problems which he was still not able to solve. For men who live in a world of sky-scrapers, motor cars and comforts of all sorts, with its varied scientific, political and social ambitions, with its desire for wealth and its highly developed system of trade and commerce, it is inevitably difficult to appreciate, or rightly understand, the minds of those who felt disinclined to all worldly things and were uneasy until they could touch their own inmost self. Theirs, however, was no ordinary pessimism, as is too often supposed by unsympathetic and shallow-minded scholars, who lack the imagination and the will to understand the Indian thought and culture of the past. They felt dissatisfied with the world not because the world had no pleasures or joys to offer, but because their desire for attaining their highest good, their true selves, was so great that it could tolerate no compromise with any other kind of desire. The sole ambition of the yogins, or the seers who practised the yoga discipline, was to become absolutely free from all kinds of bonds and from all kinds of extraneous determination.   6

The problem of how to become free naturally raised the question as to who is to become free and from what. The logic of the yogins is irresistible. It is the self which has to become free; in fact it is always free. The self is the ultimate principle of pure consciousness, distinct from all mental functions, faculties, powers, or products. By a strange, almost inexplicable, confusion we seem to lose touch with the former so that we consider it as non-existent and characterize the latter with its qualities. It is this confusion which is at the root of all our psychological processes. All mental operations involve this confusion by which they usurp the place of the principle of pure consciousness so that it is only the mind and the mental operations of thought, feeling, willing, which seem to be

existing, while the ultimate principle of consciousness
is lost sight of. If we call this ultimate principle of
consciousness, this true self, "spirit" and designate all
our functions of knowing, feeling, and willing collec-
tively as "mind," then we may say that it is only by
a strange confusion of mind with spirit that the mind
comes to the forefront and by its activities seems to
obscure the true light of the spirit. Our senses run
after their objects and the mind establishes relations
between the sense-data, or sensations, and deals with
the concepts formed therefrom as it carries on the
processes of logical thought with the aid of memory.
The external objects which draw minds to them are
not in themselves directly and immediately responsible
for obscuring the spirit or in binding it to them. It is,
rather, the mind and its activities by which the true
nature of the spirit seems to be obscured so that the
mind usurps the rightful place of the spirit. What is
necessary, therefore, is to control the activities of the
mind and to stop all mental processes. If we can in
this way kill the mind, all logical thought and all sense
processes will be killed with it. The light of the spirit
will then shine alone by itself unshadowed by the dark-
ening influence of thought. The spirit, the ultimate
principle of consciousness, and the self are one and the
same thing, the three terms expressing the threefold
aspect of its nature. But this entity, by whichever
name it is called, is to be distinguished from mind,
whose activities are thoughts, feelings, etc. We may
here employ a simile. We may say that the spirit is
like a pure white light covered by the colored dome

of the mind. This colored dome hides the pure white
light, and, without changing the nature of the white
light by its own color, makes the latter appear as colored and wrongfully appears itself to be a source of
colored light, though it has no light whatsoever of itself. We fail to recognize the white light within and
take it for granted that the colored dome is itself a
colored light. The only way to restore the purity of
the white light is by smashing the colored dome. Similarly, the only way in which the spirit may be made to
realize, in its own non-conceptual way, its own lonely
light is by breaking the mind to pieces.   7

The mind lives by its activities of sensing, perceiving
and conceiving. It creates illusions and hallucina-
tions, revives past experiences in memory, and sometimes passes into a state of sleep in which it creates
dreams. If the movement of the mind could be entirely stopped, its disintegration would be effected.
The process of yoga consists in so controlling the activity of the mind that it ceases to pass through its
different states. The cessation of all mental states is
yoga. These mental states as they rise and pass away
are not altogether lost. They continue in the subconscious mind as impressions which are revived by proper
excitations. As they are thus revived and repeated,
and return to the subconscious, the impressions become strengthened, growing more and more powerful
and more likely to occur as conscious states. Thus,
for example, when we once devote ourselves to making money and to enjoying the comforts it can pro-
cure, we become more and more deeply absorbed in

earning money and enjoying its comforts. Similarly, the scholar through days and nights of study in his library grows ever more attached to his occupation of study. It is in this way that the tendencies of the mind become strengthened; repeating themselves almost mechanically they keep alive the continual flow of the mind from one state to another. Yoga consists in stopping the conscious and sub-conscious mental flow entirely and absolutely.   8

It is easy to see that no one will think of destroying his mind unless his desire for the absolute freedom of the spirit becomes so great that all the activities of the mind, all his sense-enjoyments, all his thoughts and feelings, lose all interest for him and appear to him to be entirely valueless. This disinclination to all worldly things, called *vairagya,* is the first thing which leads the yogin to seek the way of yoga to deliver himself forever from all mundane experiences. The seer is as sensitive as the pupil of the eye. Just as a speck of dust, which passes altogether unnoticed on any other part of the body, causes great pain when it gets into the eye, so the suffering, which is absolutely unnoticed by the ordinary person, is felt keenly by the seer. All ordinary pleasures appear to be distasteful to him. There is nothing in anything worldly that can give him any satisfaction. He is in that mood in which he is dissatisfied with them all and wishes to shun them.   9

Such a state of mind cannot be produced unless the mind has risen to the highest plane of moral elevation. Unless the mind is made absolutely pure there cannot be any steady disinclination toward worldly things.

A seer must abstain from all injury to living beings. His tenderness should extend not only to all human individuals but to all living beings. He would not willfully take the life of, or injure, any living being. He would not steal the property of any other person. He would be absolutely truthful in thought, word and deed. Veracity consists in the agreement of words and thoughts with facts. But it must always be employed for the good of others and not for their injury. If it proves injurious to living beings, with whatever intention it be uttered it is not truth. Though outwardly such a truthful course may be considered virtuous yet since by his truth he has caused injury to another he has in reality violated the ideal of absolute non-injury. The seer must have a complete control of the sex tendencies. He must not desire anything more than the bare necessities. For the acquisition of things always entails attachment and greed, and injury to others in acquiring and preserving them. If in performing the great duty of universal non-injury, and in cultivating the other virtues auxiliary to it, a man be troubled by thoughts of sin, he should try to substitute for the sinful ideas those which are contrary to them. Thus, if the old habit of sin tends to drive him along the wrong path, he should, in order to banish it, entertain ideas such as the following:—"Being burnt up as I am in the fires of the world, I have taken refuge in the practice of yoga, which gives protection to all. Were I to resume the sins which I have abandoned, I should certainly be behaving like a dog which eats its own vomit—I should be acting as if I were to take up again that which I had once put aside." Thus one should habituate himself to meditation upon the harmful effects of the tendencies which are leading him along the wrong path. The habituation to this contrary tendency consists in continually thinking that these immoral tendencies cause an infinity of pain and error. Pain and error are the unending fruits of these immoral tendencies and in the recognition of this lies the power of righting the trend of our thoughts.   10

Other moral qualities of a positive character are considered indispensable to a seer toiling on the path of yoga. These are: purity, contentment, indifference to physical difficulties of heat, cold, etc., study and self-surrender to God. Purity here means both physical and mental cleanliness. Contentment means that self-satisfied condition of the mind in which we are at peace with ourselves, having ceased to run after new wants. Indifference to physical difficulties is also a virtue to be acquired by the yogin, who should be able to bear calmly the bodily wants of hunger and thirst, heat and cold. He should also be able to stop his physical movements for a considerable length of time, and be able, as well, to stop his desire to talk with others and to remain absolutely dumb.   11

In the last lecture, on the Upanishadic mysticism, it was shown that when such a high standard of moral elevation is reached and we seek to know the inmost essence of self, the self often reveals its own true nature through a direct intuition which is beyond the grasp of the mind and the senses. The yogins, how-

ever, not only emphasized the necessity of the highest
moral perfection but they also required a particular
course of physical and mental discipline as indispensable to the realization of yoga's high ideal. The yogins
emphasized not only the negative aspect of morality,
such as abstinence from injury, falsehood and the like,
but also such positive moral virtues as purity and contentment. The four cardinal virtues which a yogin was
required to possess were universal friendship (*maitri*),
compassion for all who suffer (*karuna*), happiness in
the happiness of others (*mudita*), and a sympathetic
consideration for the failings of others (*upeksha*). But
even these were not deemed sufficient; they were only
preliminary acquirements which the yogin must possess before starting with his yoga practices. The acquisition of these moral virtues went, indeed, a long
way in restraining the mind from running after sense-
objects and from being disturbed by greed, passions
and antipathies; for the yogin was self-controlled, con-
tented, pure in mind and body, and peaceable and char-
itable toward all living beings. But still he must be
able to control his bodily movements. He must therefore habituate himself to sitting in one posture for a
long time, not only for hours and days but often for
months and years together. This implied the attainment of a power to bear calmly hunger and thirst, heat
and cold, and all physical hardships.　　　　12

In order that the movement in the body may be reduced to a minimum, it is necessary to acquire a control over breathing. To practice the science of breath-
control, the yogin seats himself firmly, fixes his eyes

on an object beyond him, or rather on the tip of his own nose or on the point between his two eye-brows, and slowly inhales a full breath. At first the breath that is taken in is kept perhaps for a minute and then slowly exhaled. The practice is continued for days and months, the period of the retention of the breath taken in being gradually increased. With the growth of breath-control, one may keep his breath suspended, without exhalation or inhalation, for hours, days, months and even years together. With the suspension of the respiratory process the body remains in a state of suspended animation, without any external signs of life. The heart ceases to beat, there is neither taking in of food nor evacuation of any sort, there is no movement of the body. There is a complete cessation of the respiratory process as, with his mouth shut and his tongue turned backwards behind the tonsils stopping the passage of air firmly like a lid, the yogin sits in his fixed posture in an apparently lifeless condition. Even in modern times there are many well-attested cases of yogis who can remain in this apparently lifeless condition for more than a month. I have myself seen a case where the yogin stayed in this condition for nine days. The case of Saint Haridas is well-known. He remained buried underneath the ground for forty days under strict vigilance of guards. When, after forty days of breathless and foodless condition of suspended animation, he was brought out of the earth, there was apparently no life in him, no movement of breath, no heart-beats. But after his body had been rubbed and much water had been

poured on him he again came back to life and began
to breathe normally.   13

Various methods of purifying the body were gradually discovered by which the yogin could so temper
the body as to make it immune to diseases. In earlier
times, before the elaborate bodily disciplines had been
discovered, the yogin prayed to God and depended on
His grace for the immunity from disease which was
so necessary to the proper performance of his yoga
duties. But later on, the yogin tried to be more or
less independent of God's grace and discovered a
whole system of bodily exercises, breathing exercises,
and automatic internal washings by which his body
became so tempered that no diseases could easily at-
tack him. These consisted, first, in habituating the
body to keeping fixed postures which required various muscular movements. By this means the yogin
could make his body flexible, reduce its unnecessary
fat, and attain full control over his voluntary muscles.
For these postures required the exercise of all the voluntary muscles. Second, through the breathing exercises which could be performed in different forms
and in different degrees of intensity, combined with
the different postures, the yogin obtained control over
the various involuntary muscles which regulate the operation of the viscera, including the bladder and the
excretory organs, the heart, the stomach, etc. Added
to these was, third, the thorough washing away of the
impurities which, being secreted by some of the internal organs, obstruct their normal activity and lower
their power of resistance. These washings can be

easily performed by the control that the yogin acquires over his inner involuntary muscles. Thus, for example, the yogin can take water into the intestines by expelling air from these cavities and thus forcing in water by the downward path from a tub in which he may be sitting at the time. He can expel air from these cavities by means of the control that he has over the muscles of those organs which to a normal person are quite involuntary. Thus, at any time that he likes he can thoroughly wash his stomach, his bladder, urethra, etc. He has thus a thorough access to all the important cavities of the body where impurities may be produced and deposited. In short, by the combined operation of postures, breath-control, breathing exercises, and the voluntary washings of the impurities from all the important cavities of the body, he can so increase his power of physical resistance as to remain practically immune to all diseases.   14

But these are all merely external preparations to fit the body for the yoga practices. The real yoga practice of the mind can be properly begun only when these preliminaries have been to a large extent acquired so that the chances of external bodily disturbances and internal disturbances due to passions, antipathies, attachments, etc., have been minimized. The yogin begins this superior mental yoga by concentrating at first on any gross physical object. This concentration is not the ordinary concentration of thought as exemplified in any scientific or literary work. For this latter type of concentration consists in the limiting of the mind's activity to matters associated with the object of attention. Thus, if we concentrate on the writing of a poem or the description of scenery, what we do is to restrain the mind from flying off to other objects in which we are not interested at the time and to focus it upon the relations between various associated images and thoughts. The mind is in such cases in a lively state of movement within a limited sphere, always seeking to discover new relations or to intensify the comprehension of relations and facts already known. But yoga concentration aims not to discover any new relations or facts or to intensify any impression; it aims solely to stop the movement of mind and to prevent its natural tendency towards comparison, classification, association, assimilation and the like. The fixing of the mind on an object is done with the specific purpose of pinning it to that object and of preventing its transition to any other object. By this process the mind becomes one with the object, and so long as it is pinned to that object its movement is stopped. At the first stage of this union, there is knowledge of the name and the physical form of the object to which the mind has been pinned. But at the next stage nothing is known of the object in its ordinary relations of name and form, but the mind becomes one with the object, steady and absolutely motionless. This state is called a state of *samadhi*, or absorptive concentration. This stage arises when the mind by its steadiness becomes one with its object, divested of all associations of name and concept, so that it is in direct touch with the reality of the thing uncontaminated by associations. In this state, the object does not appear as an object of *my* consciousness but my consciousness, becoming divested of all "I" or "mine," becomes one with the object itself. There is no awareness here that "I know this," but, the mind having become one with the thing, the duality of subject and object disappears, and the result is the transformation of the mind into the object of its concentration. Our ordinary knowledge of things is full of false and illusory associations which do not communicate to us the real nature of the object; but when such an absorptive union of object and mind takes place, a new kind of intuition is produced, called *prajna,* similar to the Upanishadic intuition, called *prajnana,* and thereby the real nature of the thing is brought home to us. This *prajna* knowledge, which is a new kind of intuition produced by stopping the movement of the mind, is entirely different from the ordinary logical type of cognition of thoughts, images, etc. This intuition is a direct acquaintance, more or less similar to direct perceptual vision but free from the ordinary errors of all sense-perception. Such a steadiness can however be achieved only after continual practice. A yogin must be always watchful, particularly in the first stages, to keep his mind steadily on the object of his concentration. He must have, therefore, an inexhaustible fund of active energy (*virya*).   15

On the negative side we have, therefore, disinclination to worldly things; on the positive side, firm faith in the efficacy of the yoga process and vigorous energy exercised in steadying the mind in contemplation. Gradually, as the yogin becomes more proficient, he se-

lects subtler and finer objects for his concentration;
and at each stage in this refinement, new forms of
intuitional prajna, or yoga knowledge, dawn. With
this advancement, the yogin develops many miraculous
powers over natural objects and over the minds of
men. Truths wholly unknown to others become known
to him. Though all these powers confirm his faith
in the yoga process, he does not allow himself to be led
away by their acquisition, but steadily proceeds toward
that ultimate stage in which his mind will be disin-
tegrated and his self will shine forth in its own light
and he himself will be absolutely free in bondless,
companionless loneliness of self-illumination.   16

This *prajna*, or yoga intuitional knowledge, may be
considered as a new dimension of knowledge wholly
different from any other kind of knowledge derived
by the movement of the mind. The most fundamental
characteristic of yoga mysticism consists, on its negative side, not only in a disbelief in the ability of
sense-perception and logical thought to comprehend
the ultimate truth about the absolute purity and un-
attached character of our true self; but also in a disbelief in the possibility of the realisation of this highest truth so long as the mind itself is not destroyed.
On its positive side, it implies that intuitional wisdom
is able to effect a clear realisation of truth by gradually destroying the so-called intellect. The destruction of mind, of course, also involves the ultimate
destruction of this intuition itself. So neither the intuition nor our ordinary logical thought is able to
lead us ultimately to self-realisation. There are thus

three stages of knowledge. First, our ordinary sense-knowledge and logical thought which always deal with the world and worldly objects and which appear valueless to us when we are in spiritual exaltation and are anxious to attain the highest truth. Second, the intuitional yoga wisdom, which can only be attained when, as a result of the highest moral elevation and the yoga practices, the mind can be firmly steadied on an object so that it becomes one with that object and all its movements completely cease. This yoga wisdom gives us a direct non-conceptual vision of, or acquaintance with, the ultimate truths concerning all objects on which our minds may be concentrated; and gradually, as the yogin begins to concentrate on subtler and finer objects, such as mind, self, etc., higher and nobler truths concerning these become known to him. Though we are free to concentrate on any object whatsoever, it is desirable for the quicker attainment of our goal that we should concentrate on God—surrender ourselves to Him. In the most advanced state of this yoga intuition, all the truths regarding the nature of the true self, of the mind and of the material world and its connection with mind, become clear, and as a result of this and also as a result of the gradual weakening of the constitution of the mind, the latter ceases to live and work and is dissociated forever from the spirit or the self. It is then that the spirit shines forth in its own lonely splendor, free from the bondage of the mind which had so long by its activities led it towards false worldly attachments and to a false non-appearance of its own pure nature in all the varied products of ordinary knowledge, feeling and willing which make up our worldly life. The highest and ultimate revelation of truth is therefore not only non-conceptual and non-rational, but also non-intuitional and non-feeling. It is a self-shining which is unique. **17**

LECTURE IV
BUDDHISTIC MYSTICISM

LECTURE IV

BUDDHISTIC MYSTICISM

THE process of yoga described in the last lecture consists of a threefold course, viz., high moral elevation, physical training of the body for yoga practice, and steady mental concentration associated with the revelation of yoga wisdom, which leads to a knowledge of reality as it is. This system of thought and practice, though not without unique and distinctive features, was largely an adoption from very early times. Thus the heretical school of the Jains, which, like the Buddhistic school, holds to a monastic religion, but which was founded earlier than 500 B. C., the date of the Buddha, also considered yoga as the means of liberation of the soul. For the Jains, the liberated state of the soul is not one of pure, feelingless, non-conceptual, non-intuitional self-illumination, but is a state of supreme happiness in which the liberated self possesses a full perfection of all kinds of knowledge: perceptual, logical, alogical, intuitional and trance cognition. This liberation is attained, they believe, by the performance of yoga. Yoga with them consists mainly of a high elevation of character and complete cessation from the doing of evil, like the yoga of Patanjali described in the last lecture. They lay great emphasis on the principle of non-injury, but they also urge the necessity of the other virtues demanded by the yoga of Patanjali. Here, then, we have a system of thought according to which high moral elevation, by the cessation from all evil-doing and the acquirement of all the positive virtues is supposed to reveal a knowledge of reality as it is, and ultimately to liberate us from the bondage of our deeds and bring us to a state of perfect happiness, perfect knowledge and perfect power. The Jains, like the yogins, also believe that without the control of the mind no one can proceed in the true path. All our acts become controlled when our minds become controlled. It is by attachment and antipathy that man loses his independence. It is thus necessary for the yogin that he should be free from both attachment and antipathy and become independent in the real sense of the term. When a man learns to look upon all beings with an equal eye, he can effect such freedom, in a manner impossible even by the practice of the strictest asceticism through millions of years.   1

The Buddha himself, as the legendary account of his life tells us, once went out with his friends for a ride on horseback through the fields outside his capital. There he saw that, as the fields were being ploughed by the peasants, many insects were being mutilated and killed with each drive of the plough; and he saw also the sufferings of the poor beasts that were employed in the field. Extremely affected by these sufferings, he dismounted from his horse and sat on the grassy ground to reflect on the ultimate destiny of all beings. He realized that sufferings, diseases, old age and death are evils to which we are all subject. At that moment he saw a monk who said that, being afraid of births and deaths, he had renounced the world for his eternal salvation. The suggestion affected him very deeply. He therefore decided to renounce the world and seek to discover the way to the extinction of all sorrows, sufferings, diseases, old age and death. After testing many ways followed by other people, the Buddha himself adopted the path of yoga for the attainment of the truth that he ultimately discovered. As he sat with fixed determination he was tempted in various ways by Mara, the Buddhist Satan, but all these temptations failed and the Buddha remained firm in his purpose. 2

In the teachings and instructions found in Pali works ascribed to the Buddha, it is said that we are bound, without and within, by the entanglements of desire and that the only way of loosening these is by the practice of right discipline, concentration and wisdom. Right discipline or sila means the desisting from the commission of all sinful deeds. This is the first prerequisite. Thereby one refrains from all actions prompted by bad desires. Concentration or samadhi is a more advanced effort. By it all the roots of the old vicious tendencies and desires are destroyed, and one is led to the more advanced state of a saint. It leads directly to *prajna* or true wisdom; and by this wisdom one achieves his final emancipation. Here also, as in the yoga of Patanjali, the individual must habituate himself to meditating on the fourfold virtues of universal friendship, universal compassion, happiness in the happiness of all, and indifference to any kind of preferment, whether of himself, his friend, his enemy or a neutral party. By thus rooting out all misery he will eventually become happy; he will avoid thoughts of death and live cheerfully, and will then pass over to the idea that other beings would also fare similarly. He may in this way habituate himself to thinking that his friends, his enemies and all those with whom he is not connected might all become happy. He may fix himself in this meditation to such an extent that he obliterates all differences between the happiness of himself and that of others. He remembers that if he allows himself to be affected by anger he would weaken the self-restraint which he has been carefully practising. If some one has done a vile action by inflicting an injury, that cannot be a reason why he should himself do the same by being angry with others. If he were finding fault with others for being angry, could he himself indulge in anger? A saint who has thus made his sila or right discipline firm enters into a state of concentration which has four stages of gradual advancement. In the fourth or the last stage both happiness and misery vanish and all the roots of attachment and antipathies are destroyed. With the mastery of this stage of concentration there comes the final state of absolute extinction of the mind and of total cessation of all sorrows and sufferings—Nirvana.   3

It is easy to see that this system of yoga is very much akin to Patanjali's yoga; and it is not improbable that both Patanjali and Buddha but followed a practice which had been in existence from much earlier times, so that neither of them may be credited with its discovery. But there is one point in which there is at least a good deal of theoretical difference between Buddha's system and that of Patanjali. The ultimate goal of all concentration and its highest perfection with the Buddha is absolute extinction, while with Patanjali it is liberation of the spirit as self-illumination.   4

It is indeed very difficult to describe satisfactorily the ultimate mystical stage of Buddhistic Nirvana. For in one sense it is absolutely contentless. It is the state of deliverance from all sorrow and from all happiness. Yet, as the ultimate ideal of all our highest strivings and the goal of all our moral perfection and concentration, it was an ideal which was in the highest degree attractive to the Buddhists. Had it been conceived as pure and simple extinction or annihilation, it could not have had the attraction for the Buddhists that it did. In many passages it is actually described as blissful. In other passages it is held to be like the extinction of a flame. Some European scholars have considered the descriptions of Nirvana by the Buddhists to be incoherent or inconsistent. It is not surprising that European scholars, who are temperamentally often very different from the Buddhists of India, should fall into error in trying to comprehend the mystical state of Nirvana. Whether we read the teachings of the Upanishads or of the yoga of Patanjali, the ultimate state representing the goal of all the spiritual quest and spiritual strivings of the sages is set forth as absolutely contentless and non-conceptual. It is the self no doubt, but this self is entirely different from the self with which we are familiar in all our ordinary worldly concerns. It is the extinction of all our sorrows and pleasures and all our worldly experiences as much as is Nirvana. It is a state of absolute dissolution of all world-process. Though a blissful state, there is no distinction here between the bliss and the enjoyer of the bliss. But still it is just such a non-logical ultimate state that could stimulate the highest strivings of the best men of India. To call it blissful is not to understand bliss in an ordinary way. For this mystical bliss is incomprehensible by the intellect. 5

Nirvana was conceived as a state similar to that just described. If it was compared to the extinction of a flame, this was quite proper. For is it not a state in which all worldly experiences entirely and absolutely cease to exist? Yet it is blissful in the sense that it can stimulate our spiritual cravings and spiritual strivings to the highest degree. The Hindus thought that at this state there is only the self-luminous self. The Buddhists, however, could not say what exists at this state for they denied the existence of the self. But the teaching of the Hindus is scarcely more comprehensible, except for the fact that at least from the grammatical and literary point of view we have in "the self-luminous self" a positive expression. But this self is as indescribable as is the state of Nirvana, except by the negative method of "not this," "not that." But still this state was rightfully called immortal and blissful because it was looked upon by the Buddhists as

the end of all their sufferings, the goal of all their spiritual strivings, and the culmination of spiritual perfection. What is especially emphasized, from the negative
point of view, is that it is absolutely non-logical in its
nature. It has no describable essence. The mysticism
of the Buddhist consists in a belief in this essenceless
state of Nirvana' as the state of ultimate perfection
and ultimate extinction, to be realized by the complete extinction of desires and the supra-intellectual
wisdom of the yoga practice.   6

So, though, for academic and philosophical discussions, the essenceless state of the vacuity of Nirvana
is absolutely different from the pure self of yoga liberation, yet from the point of view of mystical experience both are too deep and unfathomable for ordinary
comprehension. Both are transcendent, unworldly,
and contentless in their nature; and the methods of
their realization are also largely similar.   7

In digressing, I shall now turn your attention to
other forms of mysticism inviting a belief in non-logical
methods of achieving one's highest goal of power, happiness, wisdom or emancipation, and shall speak of
Indian asceticism. The Taittiriya Brahmana, which
was composed probably as early as 700 B. C. (if not
even earlier) speaks of Brahmacharya in the sense
of studying the Vedas with due self-control. We find
there the story of Bharadvaja who practised Brahmacharya for one whole life which was as long as three

---

[1] There are some Buddhist thinkers, the Sthiramati, who hold
that the state of Nirvana is a state of subject-object-less, pure,
unchangeable consciousness called atayvignana.

lives. Indra approached him and, finding him decayed
and old, said, "Bharadvaja, if I were to give you a
fourth life, what would you do with it?" He an-
swered, "I would use it in practising Brahmacharya."
The word *tapas* etymologically means heat, and in the
Atharva Veda (XVII. 1. 24) is actually used in the
sense of the heat of the sun. But by an extension of
meaning the word was used to denote also the exertion
of mental energy for the performance of an action
and for the endurance of privations of all kinds, of
heat, cold, and the like. It was regarded as a great
force which could achieve extraordinary results. Thus
it is said in the Taittiriya Upanishad that the Great
Being performed *tapas* and having done so created all
the world. In Rig Veda (X. 167. 1) Indra is said to
have gained Heaven by *tapas*. *Tapas* was thus probably understood from very early times as some kind
of austere discipline, the exact nature of which, however, was rather vague, changeable and undefined.   8

In Ashvaghosha's Buddhacharita, which was written
probably during the first century of the Christian era,
we find that the Buddha was told by an ascetic in the
forest how different ascetics lived like birds, by pick-
ing up grains left in the fields; others ate grass like
animals; some lived with snakes; some sat still, like
ant-hills, with nests of birds in the tangles of their
long hair and snakes playing on their bodies; some
lived in water, with tortoises eating parts of their bodies, thinking that misery itself is virtue and that the
highest happiness in Heaven can be achieved by under-
going sufferings of all kinds. Even in recent times In-

dian ascetics have inflicted on themselves various kinds of self-mortifications for the merits that are supposed to be derived from them. Thus a Brahmin ascetic at Benares is known to have lived for thirty-five years on a flat board studded with iron nails or spikes on which he sits and lies down at full length and which he never leaves night or day. Another common form of self-torture is to raise one or both arms above the head, and to hold them there until they become stiff and atrophied. Some ascetics are known to live with four fires burning very near them on their four sides and with the sun shining over their heads. Others undertake prolonged fastings and take vows of silence for years.   9

We read in the Puranas that self-mortification by itself was believed to generate a force. By virtue of the force, power or energy of these self-mortifications, an ascetic who performed them could exact from the god he worshipped, any boon that he wanted and the god could not refuse to grant him the boon even though he knew that the effect of granting it would be seriously mischievous. In the Ramayana, the greatest epic of India, the story is told of Ravana, the great demon who carried away Sita, the wife of Rama. Ravana had won the boon from Prajapati that he could not be killed by gods or demons, and it was by virtue of this boon that he could conquer all the gods, though he was ultimately killed by Rama, a man. A story is told of a demon who had a boon from the god Shiva that the person on whose head he would put his hands would be reduced to ashes. When the boon was granted, the demon wanted to test its truth by putting his hands on the head of the god Shiva himself. Shiva was very much afraid and started to fly away with the demon pursuing him in hot haste. But the god Shiva had no power of taking away the favor that he had granted, for it was earned by the force of the *tapas* of the demon. Vishnu, who came to rescue the god Shiva, played a trick upon the demon. The latter was asked to test the truth of the boon about which he was sceptical on his own head and thus he was reduced to ashes. This *tapas* is often described as a fire. Unless the boon is granted and the ascetic desists from his *tapas,* it is believed that the fire of his *tapas* might even burn the whole world as it were. The force of these stories is that there was a belief that self-mortification is itself a source of great power and that by it one could gain any desire, be it an immortal life in Heaven, the conquest of all the worlds, or any other fanciful desire—even the liberation from all bondage. We thus find that, just as in the Vedic school sacrifice was conceived as a power which could produce any beneficial results that the sacrificer wanted, so in this Puranic school there was the belief that *tapas* as self-mortification could give an individual anything he craved. It was a power by itself. These *tapas* performances were apparently carried out to please certain gods, just as oblations were offered to the Vedic gods in sacrifices; yet the god with reference to whom the *tapas* was performed had no power to refuse the boon. The boons were exacted from the gods by the power of *tapas,* whether or not the gods

willed to grant them of their own free volition, just
as the effects of sacrifice did not in any way depend on
the good will of the gods to whom offerings were made
at those sacrifices.   10

We know that *tapas* as the power of endurance of
physical privations and troubles was an indispensable
accessory of both the Buddhist yoga and Patanjali's
yoga. The gradual abandonment of desires until their
ultimate extinction could be effected, was essential both
to yoga and to Buddhism. It is true that the Upanishads do not speak of the extinction of desires, but
they certainly praise self-control as an indispensable
desideratum. There is indeed the law of karma which
requires that every person reap the fruits of his actions, whether good or bad, and that if the life of the
present birth is not sufficient for the experience of the
sufferings or the joys which are put to his account in
accordance with the measure of his vice or virtue, he
will enjoy or suffer the fruits of his deeds in another
birth. So, in an endless chain of births and rebirths,
moves on the cyclic destiny of man. All his rebirths
are due to the fact that he is filled with desires, and
for their fulfillment he performs actions out of attachments, passions, antipathies, etc. By the law of
karma (which acts automatically according to some,
and is controlled by the will of God according to
others) he enjoys or suffers the fruits of his actions
in this or in subsequent births. So if the successive
chain of births is to be terminated, the accretion of
the fruits of karma must be stopped, and if the
accretion of karma is to be stopped, desire must be

rooted out. I shall not enter into the subtle question as to whether the place of superior importance belongs to karma or to the extinction of desires in the Hindu, Buddhist and Jaina schemes of life. Whichever of the two may be considered the more important in each particular Hindu or Buddhist system of thought, they are nevertheless indissolubly connected. For out of desires come the actions and their fruits, and out of actions and the enjoyment or suffering of their fruits of pleasures or sorrows come further desires, and so on. However, if one looks at the matter psychologically, the extinction of desires may be considered the more important, since it is for Indian philosophy the indispensable ethical desideratum for all spiritual achievement. If the ultimate freedom of the spirit and the cessation of the cycle of births and rebirths be the ultimate ethical and spiritual goal, this can only be attained by the extinction of desires and the termination of the accretion of the fruits of our deeds. The development of the ideal of *tapas* is a direct result of this ideal of the extinction of desires. It was probably thought in some circles that control of desires implies on its positive side the idea of self-mortification. Logically it certainly does not. But the mistaken transition is easy. So there grew up a system of practice in which people thought that self-mortifications are of the highest merit and are capable of giving anything that might be desired. Soon degeneration set in. Self-mortifications were probably introduced as supplementary to the control of desires. They then came to be practiced for the indulgence of desires for attaining heaven or superior power, and thus began to perform functions similar to those that were ascribed to sacrifices in Vedic circles.   11

The Buddha himself, as the legendary account of Ashvaghosha's Buddhacharita relates, directs the same criticisms as the above against the practice of self-mortification. He deplores the fact that, after leaving all worldly comforts, relatives and friends, men should with all these self-mortifications called tapas, desire only the satisfaction of desires. People are afraid of death, but when they seek the satisfaction of desires this leads to births, and thus they again face death of which they are afraid. If self-mortification is by itself productive of virtue, then the enjoyment of pleasures must be vicious. But if it is believed that virtue produces pleasures or happiness, and if pleasures are vices, then virtue produces vice, which is self-contradictory. It is strange, however, that the Buddha himself, when he wanted to attain to the highest wisdom or philosophy, undertook for six years the most rigorous asceticism and with all his limbs emaciated was almost on the point of death. He did not, of course, aim at the fruition of any ordinary desires, but at the discovery of the wisdom by which birth and death and all the sufferings associated with them could be stopped. All the same, he at first followed the custom then prevalent among ascetics and underwent the most austere discipline. But at the end of six years he realized that the performance of asceticism was unnecessary and without value for the attainment of the higher wisdom. He then bethought himself as to how he might regain his former strength and physique.

He thought that by hunger, thirst and fatigue the mind loses its ease, and that if the mind is not at ease one cannot by its use attain the highest wisdom. It is by the due satisfaction of the senses that the mind comes to its ease, and it is the easy, peaceful, and healthy mind in a healthy body that can attain the wisdom of yoga concentration. So the Buddha gave up his old forms of hard ascetic practice and tried to regain his health by proper food, bathing, etc. His associates, however, who probably knew only the old forms of practice, and were therefore shocked over his abandonment of them, left him. It was only after he had thus recovered his health that he could resist all the temptations of Mara, the Buddhistic Satan, and attain by concentration, highest wisdom. The wisdom that the Buddha attained seems to have been more of the nature of logical thought, but the goal that was to be attained by such wisdom was the mystical, inexpressible, essenceless Nirvana; and the direct means by which this could be attained was not logical thought or reasoning or scriptural or other kinds of learning, but the extinction of all desires (*trishna-kshaya*). [12]

The principal virtues of universal friendship, universal compassion, etc., to which reference has already been made, were appreciated early in Buddhism and also in the yoga of Patanjali. But it may well be argued that there was scarcely any place for the active manifestation of universal friendship or universal compassion in a scheme of life which was decidedly individualistic. No one who sought the absolute freedom of his own self, or the extinction of his whole personality like the extinguishing of a flame, and who sought the cessation of his own rebirths and sorrow as the only goal and the only ambition to be realized, could have much scope for any active manifestation of universal friendship. The altruistic ideal can therefore at best be merely a disposition, and can manifest itself merely in a negative way, e. g., in non-injury to any being. But a person who holds such an individualistic notion of salvation cannot, in his scheme of life, have any leisure or opportunity for the doing of active good to others. [13]

In the Hindu Puranas or religio-mythological works, written in poetry, we sometimes come across tales of wonderful self-sacrifice for the good of the gods or even for the good of animals who sought protection. But tales of self-sacrifice from the motive of universal friendship are very rare, and they do not seem to fit in with the Hindu ideal of personal and individual liberation. A story is told that when the gods were in great trouble in their war with Vritra, a demon, they approached the sage Dadhichi. For it was decreed by fate that the demon could be killed with a weapon made of Dadhichi's bones but with nothing else. Dadhichi, in response to the request of the gods, willingly gave up his life, in order that the gods, with a weapon made of his bones, might destroy the demon. A story is also told of King Shibi, who was tested by the gods Indra and Agni. Agni took the form of a pigeon, and Indra that of a pursuing hawk. The pigeon took shelter with King Shibi. The latter

would not give it over to the hawk because the pigeon
had taken shelter with him and under these circumstances he would rather give up his own life than allow
the pigeon to be killed. At last the hawk said that he
would be satisfied if King Shibi would give from his
own body flesh of the same weight as that of the pigeon, and the king cut the flesh of his thigh with his
own sword. This, however, is a case of the kshatriya's
virtue of giving shelter to those who seek it, even at
the sacrifice of one's own life. It does not exemplify
self-sacrifice for the good of beings in general, out of
pure motives of universal friendship. The tale is a
Brahmanic adaptation of a Buddhist story called Shi-
bijataka, in which King Shibi is said to have torn out
his eyes and made a gift of them out of motives of
pure charity alone. In another story in the Mahabharata, Shibi is said to have cut up his own son as food
for a Brahmin who desired the son's flesh for dinner; and to please the Brahmin Shibi was prepared
to join in eating the dinner consisting of his own son's
flesh. The motive here was the supreme duty of pleasing the Brahmins and giving them whatever they
wanted.   14

But though the ideal of universal friendship and
compassion does not seem to have been an active creed
among the Hindus or among the followers of the Hin-
ayana school of early Buddhism, it assumed a rôle of
paramount importance in the Mahayana school of
Buddhism. Here universal altruism and universal
compassion, and happiness and sorrow in the happiness and sorrow of others, form the dominant prin-

ciple. The philosophy of the Mahayana Buddhism was peculiarly idealistic. It taught that matter as such has no existence in any form, and that all things perceived are but creations of the mind, and more like a magic show than reality. Everything, according to it, is essenceless and indescribable, mere phantom creation of the mind. Indeed, mind itself is not ultimately real in any sense, but is as illusory a creation as all other things created by it. It is the realization of this that was called *bodhi* or perfect knowledge. Those who perceive this truth attain perfect knowledge and, like a flame extinguished, reach Nirvana or the final deliverance from all sorrows and rebirths. [15]

There is a lower order of saints called *arhats,* or *pratyekabuddhas.* These *pratyekabuddha* saints are said to be of a lower order because they live alone by themselves like the rhinoceros. By their spiritual endeavors, they obtain a logical understanding of the way in which all worldly things originate and pass away; and by meditation on the essencelessness of all things, they attain perfect knowledge and Nirvana. They are not instructed by any one, nor do they teach others to attain the knowledge that they gain. They are accustomed from the beginning to lead a lonely life like the Hindu yogis, and the instruction of others does not interest them. They are therefore regarded as being only Buddhas or enlightened ones of a lower order.

The higher Buddhas are those who aim not only at the vision of truth for destroying their inner notion of self or ego and all desires of existence and non-existence, but also at doing good to all living beings and constantly practicing the great virtues. Their enlightenment includes not only the possession of the truth indispensable to salvation, but also omniscience, universal knowledge of all details of things, and omnipotence. The perfect Buddha attains these powers not only through his prolonged meditations, by which he gets insight into the principles of all things, but also through his infinite merits of constantly performing the great virtues of charity, patience, etc. The man who aims at the attainment of this superior Buddhahood is called a Bodhisattva (one who is on the way to the attainment of perfect knowledge). His superior aim consists in this that, at the cost of personal sufferings, he wishes the temporal happiness of others. He continually desires for others supreme and temporal happiness, and for himself the Buddhahood as a means of realizing this service to others. Even after the saint attains true enlightenment and knows that there is no essence in anything and that nothing exists, he continues to practice the virtues of charity, morality and patience, and to mature the qualities of his supreme enlightenment.   16

We sometimes hear very remarkable stories of Buddhist saints, even of actual historical saints, who showed supreme self-control and compassion for others. Thus it is said of Aryadeva, a great Buddhist teacher of the second century, that he once defeated in argument a teacher of non-Buddhistic doctrines. A young disciple of this defeated teacher, greatly enraged over his teacher's defeat, determined to murder Arya-

deva and awaited a suitable opportunity. One day
Aryadeva was preaching the doctrine of the essencelessness of all things, and was refuting heretical views
before his pupils in a solitary forest. After this instruction, while he was taking a walk alone, the enemy
stabbed him from ambush, saying, "You conquered
my teacher with your knowledge, but I now conquer
you with my sword." Aryadeva, holding fast with
his hands his stabbed belly, bade the would-be assassin
take his three clothes and bowl and escape over the
mountains in monk's garb so that others might not
capture and punish him. He further told him that
he was very sorry for him because of the seeds of
sinful deeds that he was sowing. The murderer was
deeply moved by the saint's compassion and sympathy,
and asked Aryadeva to teach him the doctrine. Even
in his wounded condition Aryadeva began to teach him
the Buddhist doctrine of the essencelessness of all
things. After giving him some instructions Aryadeva
fell in a swoon and his assailant escaped. Soon after-
wards Aryadeva's pupils came and enquired about the
murderer. To them the teacher replied that there was
no one who was killed or who killed, no friend and no
enemy, no murderer, that everything was a delusion
due to ignorance.   17

He who is kind and good and has a great propen-
sity for doing good to others, and who, though incapable of committing a sinful action for himself, may
yet be so moved by love for his fellow beings as to
commit a wrong action for them, is fit to take the vow
of a Bodhisattva who would spend all his future career

for the good of others. His enthusiasm is not for the egoistical calm of the saint who is anxious for his own deliverance; he is moved by the most altruistic of all motives, viz., compassion for all creatures. It is such a person who takes the vow of Bodhisattva or one who aspires to the goal of a future Buddha.

But even then it is one thing to take a vow and another thing to fulfil it. Ordinarily one's unconstrained love is given to himself and it is only by reflection that the Bodhisattva learns to care wholly for the welfare of others. At the lower stages, his nature leaves him at the mercy of his inclination; his knowledge of truth is but slight, and the direct penetrating sight of the yoga meditations is entirely lacking to him. But by a continual repetition of his high aspirations, and by a more and more studious practice of the good works which they involve, he gradually comes to the higher stages of progress. As he enters these, wishing to bear the burden of the sins of all human beings in the hells and elsewhere, he becomes free from all fears of evil reputation, rebirth, death, etc. Becoming more and more perfect, he gradually masters the virtues of faith, compassion, affection for all, disinterestedness, reverence for self and for others. All his actions are for the good of others, and his only thought is that he may be serviceable to all beings.   18

The person who intends to enter upon the higher career of a Bodhisattva and ultimately to become the perfect Buddha, places himself under the guidance of a religious preceptor, performs the moral or pious works, and undertakes the vow of *bodhi*. He thinks that it is only by a desire to become a perfect Buddha for the salvation of men, and by dedicating himself to the good of all beings, that the sins of his past lives can be wholly removed. He confesses his own guilt and imperfections and deplores them. He wishes to dedicate all the fruits of his virtuous deeds, merit and piety to the good of all creatures and for the attainment of their Bodhi. He wishes to be the bread for those who are hungry, and the drink for those who are thirsty. He devotes himself by his love to all beings; and in his compassion for their sufferings, he gives all that he is, to all creatures. It is by such determinations that he produces in himself the proper state of mind with which one may start in the high career of a Bodhisattva. He has then to keep a strict vigilance over his thoughts and over the resolutions that he has taken, and keep a continued watchfulness over mind and body. He must also perform the great virtues called *paramitas,* for thinking, though good in itself, is not enough by itself; it must be continually supplemented by the exercise of the great virtues. He should restrain himself from all evil by continued watchfulness over his mind and body, and by self-control attained in this way. But he must also continually perform the great virtues in order to strengthen his life in progressive good.

One of the most important of these virtues is that of giving due scope to compassion (*karuna*). The aspirant thinks that his neighbor suffers pain as he suffers his. Why should he be anxious about himself and not about his neighbor? Such a man may even commit a sin if he knows that this will be beneficial to one of his fellow-beings. For the sake of doing good to others he should always be prepared to abandon even his meditations or even his chastity. It is through this universal compassion that he can reconcile all beings to himself—by almsgiving, amiability, obligingness, and sharing the joy and sorrow of others. But he ought also to take care that his tendency to charity do not become so excessive as to stand in the way of his spiritual advancement. For it is only on a high stage of spirituality that he can make himself most genuinely serviceable to others. To give even one's flesh and blood for the good of others is good, but the giving of spiritual food is certainly better. It is not good to sacrifice one's body to satisfy the appetite of a tiger when that body in a sound condition can be utilized for giving spiritual instruction to others. 19

Careful adherence to morality, consisting of purity of intention, reformation after transgression, and regard for the law of right conduct, is another of the important conditions which a Bodhisattva should strictly meet. Without going into any details, the main principle of morality consists in abstaining from all actions hurtful to others, or the maxim, "Do not do to others what you would not like others to do unto you." But apart from this negative virtue of abstention, he should also acquire the positive virtues of devotion to study, reflection and meditation, reverence to the teacher, nursing the sick, confession of guilt, association with people in their good and useful undertakings and in their difficulties and sicknesses, giving them right teaching, etc.,—in short, doing good to all people in all possible ways.

Another important virtue is patience or control of anger, for anger is the greatest of all sins. He should also practice the virtue of energetically conquering all incapacity of body and mind, all attachment to pleasures and want of firm determination. This he can do by thinking of the evil effects of these traits and by recalling that, unless he can firmly keep himself to the strict path of virtue, he will never be able to cross the ocean of suffering, and that, however low may be his present state, he may by continued exertion raise himself to the highest stage of perfection of the Buddhas. He should also derive additional strength by thinking: first, of his great desire to rid himself and all other beings from all their sins: second, of his great pride over undertaking to bear the burdens of all creatures; third, of his joy in undertaking new tasks as soon as the old ones are finished—his happiness is in action itself, and he seeks in action no other fruit than the pleasure of the action done; fourth, of his self-mastery of attention, and of keeping his mind and body always completely alert. If he for any reason fails once, he must discover the cause and see that he may not fail again.   20

Two further virtues are contemplation or concentration and the true wisdom which realizes the nothingness of all things. It is surprising how a metaphysics of extreme idealism, of the nothingness and essencelessness of all things, or of nihilism, could set for the achievement of the highest spiritual perfection a program of life and endeavor which is altruistic in the most extreme degree imaginable. What is required is a state of perfection in which the individual esteems the ultimate state of mystical deliverance—Nirvana or extinction—to be of little consequence, and is prepared to undergo all troubles, and refuse to enter Nirvana, unless and until all beings become good and happy and come to the path of deliverance. Out of the doctrines of self-control and the ideal of the extinction of desires, there has thus come a scheme of life in which desirelessness is attained by magnifying the scope of desires from the individual to the universal, by rejecting personal good for the sake of the good of others. This good is not sought with a view to any selfish aims, for the seer knows that nothing exists and that all forms and names are empty and essenceless. But he takes it upon himself to do this because of his supreme compassion and of his determination to devote himself to the service of his fellow-beings and to bring to them the light of perfection. The milk of human kindness flows through him, and it is this flow of kindness in him which leads him to his highest perfection. With him, as Shantideva (a great authority) says, even contemplation occupies only a lower place. For he attains to his highest only by persisting in the path of compassion.

The two cardinal features of his conduct are a firm conviction of the equality of his self with that of his neighbor and the substitution of his neighbor's self for his self. Each of these features involves a clear insight into the nature of things. If with great strength one can duly exemplify them, he attains all the merits of a Bodhisattva. He understands that our only enemy is our selfish "ego." Thus, he speaks to his own self, "Renounce, O my thought, the foolish hope that I have still a special interest in you. I have given you to my neighbor, thinking nothing of your sufferings. For if I were so foolish as not to give you over to the creatures, there is no doubt that you would deliver me to the demons, the guardians of hell. How often, indeed, have you not handed me over to those wretches, and for what long tortures! I remember your long enmity, and I crush you, O self, the slave of your own interests. If I really love myself, I must not love myself. If I wish to preserve myself, I must not preserve myself."[2]

21

[2] L. de la Vallée Poussin's article *"Bodhisattva,"* *Encyclopaedia of Religion and Ethics* (edited by James Hastings), Vol. II, p. 753.

LECTURE V
CLASSICAL FORMS OF DEVOTIONAL MYSTICISM

LECTURE V

CLASSICAL FORMS OF DEVOTIONAL MYSTICISM

WE have described the ideal of supreme self-control and of the extinction of all desires as an indispensable requirement for the attainment of high perfection. This end is believed to be reached by replacing egoism with unlimited universalism, the individual learning to desire his own good by desiring the good of others. But such an unlimited universalism could hardly be practiced within the limited sphere of the duties and activities of a householder. The ideal yogin who renounced the world and spent a life of supreme self-control and suppression of all desires, and who practiced his yoga courses in which all movements of his body are inhibited, could not live in society and follow the ordinary vocations of life. Cut off from society, he pursued a goal of individualistic perfection. 1

But the general Hindu system of life was not monistic, individualistic, or separatistic. Hindu society was divided into four castes. We find (1) Brahmins, who followed the scholarly and the priestly line of work, studied the Vedas, gave spiritual instruction and performed the sacrifices; (2) Kshatriyas, the war-

113

rior caste who protected the weak from the attacks of the strong, governed kingdoms as kings, and gave to the Brahmins all protection and encouragement in their scholarly and priestly works; (3) Vaishyas, or the trading and pastoral caste, who increased the wealth of the country by trading and farming; and (4) Shudras, or the servant caste, recruited from the non-Aryans who found a home in the Aryan societies and served as menials to the Brahmins, Kshatriyas and Vaishyas.

The Brahmin went to live with his teacher from the age of eight and remained with him until he had completed the study of the Vedas. He then returned from the house of his teacher and was bound according to the injunction of the scriptures to get married, to perform regularly the sacrifices, to be united with his wife and procreate sons, to teach students, and to make gifts or charities to proper persons at auspicious times and at holy places. Upon reaching the age of fifty he had to retire to forest life with his wife, and give himself up to holy thoughts and the leading of a holy life. In the last stage of his life, it was necessary for him to renounce even his forest life of retirement. He had to sever himself from all his attachments, lead the life of a hermit and get his food by begging. Of these four stages of life, called Brahmacharya, Grihastha, Vanaprastha, and Yati, the householder's life was regarded as the best. For this stage (*ashrama*) provided an opporunity for the doing of good to the people of all the other stages of life, by gifts, by the performance of sacrifices, by instruction to teachers, and by the procreation of good sons who might become the future supporters of society. Performance of sacrifices, teaching, and the procreation of sons were regarded as debts with which every Brahmin was born, and no Brahmin had any right to seek the individualistic goal of a hermit's life unless and until he had discharged these duties for the major portion of his life. 2

Similarly, it was regarded as the duty of a Kshatriya to protect the weak and to fight in a good cause, and of a Vaisya to carry on trading and farming. The performance of the class of duties belonging to each caste at its specific stage of life is the imperative duty (*dharma*); transgression of it was held to be transgression of duty and hence vicious (*adharma*). What was expected of every man was that he follow the specific duties allotted to his caste, satisfy his desires of life, and enjoy the pleasures of life. It was a balance in which equal attention was paid to the performance of the allotted duties and to the satisfaction of personal needs and desires that was regarded as the true ideal of life for all normal persons. Only in exceptional cases did the Hindu scheme of life admit the renouncement of this life (*trivarga*) of threefold duties in a search for the attainment of the goal of liberation (*apavarga*). The yearning after a higher life was an actual and soul-stirring experience among spiritually-minded persons. They were allowed the privilege of renouncing the life of ordinary pleasures, and of seeking to kill all other desires and to attain true knowledge, by intuition, moral elevation, yoga or even by asceticism. In their case alone, however, was this exception made. But even then the exception was not very readily admitted in orthodox Hindu circles. We remember the great effort that Shankara, the great Vedanta teacher, had to make, especially in his commentary on the Gita, to establish this point. He taught that those who attained higher knowledge (*jnana*) were exempt from the allotted duties of ordinary persons. These duties were obligatory only for those who did not attain the higher knowledge. But Shankara's interpretation of the Gita was objected to by other authorities. 3

The Gita is a work of great sanctity and popularity among the Hindus. It consists of seven hundred simple verses, of which the first chapter of forty-six verses forms the introduction. It is written in the form of a dialogue between Lord Krishna and Arjuna, the great warrior who, on the battlefield of the terrible Indian civil war described in the classic heroic poem Mahabharata, is appalled at the prospect of the fearful impending destruction and refuses to fight. Lord Krishna tries to persuade him, in the Gita, that as a Kshatriya, (a man of the military caste) it is his duty to fight. To add strength to his persuasion he makes use of many moral and religious arguments. Traditionally this theme forms a part of the fifth canto of the Mahabharata. Though its date is uncertain, it may well be believed to have been written about the second or the third century B. C. It discards self-mortification and believes in three kinds of *tapas*: first, bodily discipline—respect to gods, Brahmins and the wise, purity, sincerity, chastity and non-injury; second, speech discipline—sweet and truthful speech, and study; and third, mental discipline—contentment, self-control, amiability, purity of mind, and meditation.

But the great solution of the Gita is the compromise it advances between the worldly life of allotted duties and the hermit life of absolute renouncement, and between a life of lawful and proper enjoyment and the absolute extinction of desires. The program that it proposes is, on the one hand, that we purify our minds, purging them of all attachments and passions by dedicating all the fruits of our actions to God; and yet, on the other hand, that we continue to perform all the duties belonging to our particular caste or stage of life. It is not the actions but our own inclinations and passions that really bind us. But if we can augment our faith in and our affection for God to such an extent that in our love for Him we free ourselves from all other attachments while yet we continue to perform the allotted and normal duties, the actions can in no wise bind us to a lower goal. A life dedicated to God, and lived for and in love of Him, is a life which is inevitably ennobled to the highest degree. A seer who has been able to liberate himself from the tendency to self-seeking and from attachment is never over-pleased at any good fortune nor over-sorry at any misfortune. His is a calm and unruffled life. He takes the pleasures and sorrows of life without the least perturbation; he has no fear and no anger; he is firm in himself, unshakeable and unmoved. Yet he follows the daily routine of social and other duties.

The Gita seems to reject the doctrine that the body and mind may be made entirely motionless or inactive. Simple physical conditions could make the body move; and it urges that it is only a false show of morality when the body is controlled and yet one continues to think of doing bad things or to harbor thoughts of attachment. The mysticism of the Gita consists in the belief that the performance of actions without personal attachment or self-seeking motive, and with a dedication of their fruits to God, leads a man to his highest realization or liberation. Knowledge is praised, but only because true knowledge is conducive to the acceptance of such a life of desireless self-surrender to God. A man who has no personal motive in an action really does not perform the action though to all appearances he may seem to be so doing. It is only such a person who my truly be called a yogin. His is a mind that is constantly fixed on God, and he performs all his duties for the sake of duty, out of reverence to the law, and with complete self-surrender to God. 4

Self-surrender to God, or self-abnegation, however, does not in the Gita involve a personal relationship of communion and love so much as it does the moral qualities of compassion, universal friendship, humility, contentment, want of attachment, self-control and purity. The expectation is emphasized that a person possessed of these moral qualities will be equally unruffled in sorrow and in happiness and that he will be the friend of all. Mind and intellect are to be concentrated on God, and all actions are to be surrendered to Him. This does not necessarily mean a superabundance of love. It may be an offshoot of the old yoga ideal of Patanjali. Here it is enjoined that the mind and intellect be concentrated on God, for, if this is done, God, being satisfied by this attachment, will help the yogin, and by His divine grace the yogin may achieve his goal much more easily than would otherwise be possible. The idea of the surrender of all actions to God is also to be found in the yoga of Patanjali. Though the writer of the Gita admits breath-control as a discipline, yet his whole emphasis is laid on self-abnegation and self-surrender to God. Breath-control seems to be given only a subordinate value, that of a means of purifying the mind. We have, therefore, in the Gita a new solution of how a man may attain his highest liberation. He may remain a member of society and perform his allotted duties provided he has the right sort of moral elevation, has fixed his mind on God, has dissociated himself from all attachment, and, by self-surrender and self-abnegation, has devoted himself to God. It is faith in the special grace of God to those who have surrendered themselves to Him that forms the essence of the Gita   5

Though the idea of love for God does not show itself in any prominent way in early Sanskrit literature, except in the Pancaratra literature, it is very improbable that the idea was not known from very early times. For some of the monotheistic Vedic hymns reveal an intimate personal relation with the deity, implying affection; and in the Buddhist literature we find frequent references to love for the Buddha.

In the Vishnu Purana we are given the story of Prahlada. Because of his devotion to Hari, his father tormented him in various ways and sought to put him to death by throwing him into fire or into the sea, by administering poison, and by various other methods. But he was saved from all these perils by the grace of Hari, and as a true devotee of the great Lord he was not in the least angry with his father. In all the adoration to Hari, whether on the part of Prahlada or as otherwise reported in the Vishnu Purana and in many of the other early Puranas, the great Lord is adored and praised metaphysically or philosophically as the great Being from whom everything has come forth and to whom everything will return, as the great controller of the universe and the great lord who is residing within us and is controlling us, and as the prime mover of the material cosmic world which is only a manifestation of his power. The subtle and primal cosmic matter is a concrete expression of the energy of the Lord. By His will it is set in active operation and transforms itself into the visible universe. The universe, therefore, though in a sense different from Him, is ultimately sustained and supported by Him; created by Him, it will ultimately return to Him. Many are the hymns in the Puranas which praise God in this philosophical manner and extol His great powers. There are also numberless instances in which God is said to be pleased by philosophic meditation, and in consequence appears to the devotee, to speak with him, and to grant him the boon he seeks.   6

The earlier literature does not always emphasize the feeling element in devotion. In the Vishnu Purana, however, we find that when God came face to face with Prahlada and asked him if he had a boon to crave, he besought the same attachment for the Lord that ordinary people have for sense enjoyments. The devotion that Prahlada had previously shown was a concentration on God and a serene contemplation in which he became one, as it were, with the Lord. Ramanuja, the great Vedanta commentator of the 11th century, also defines devotion (bhakti) as a contemplation of God unbroken as the smooth and ceaseless flow of oil. But that such a contemplation necessarily implies love of God as its inner motive cannot be denied, and Ramanuja also describes this ceaseless contemplation as having its main source in love for God, who was so dear to the devotee. But all that I wish to point out in this connection is that, in this aspect of devotion, contemplation and communion are more prominent than any exuberance of feeling. Prahlada was attached to God by his love of Him; God was the dearest of all dear things to him. It was this inmost and most deep-seated love for God that stirred him to withdraw his mind from all other things and to enter into such a contemplation of God that he became absorbed in Him, his whole personality lost in an ecstatic trance unity with God. But this did not satisfy Prahlada. He desired such a devotion to God that the very thought of Him would bring the same sort of satis-

faction that persons ordinarily have in thinking of
sense-objects. He desired not only contemplative
union but longed also to taste God's love as one tastes
the pleasures of the senses.   7

It is the contemplative union with God that we find
in the Gita, and the transition to it from the state of
yoga concentration is not difficult to understand. Self-
surrender to God, the higher moral elevation, and concentration on God are all present in Patanjali's yoga.
But here the objective was the destruction of the mind
through psychical exercises accompanied by the complete inhibition of bodily and mental activity. Later
the devotee seeks to attain liberation through the special grace of the Lord, which he can hope to acquire
by such contemplative union.

In later Indian thought the method of yoga on the
one hand receded in favor of that of bhakti or devotion; on the other hand, its pure form became greatly
complicated by the development of many mysterious
doctrines and rites which became associated with it,
sought its support, and claimed to be forms of it. But
my time is limited and I cannot enter into these latter
forms of mysticism. Nor can I describe those mystical religious movements which, arising as a reaction
against the dominant religious ideal of extreme sense-
control and the practice of desirelessness, tried to for-
mulate certain principles and methods by which one
could attain his highest goal not by sense-control but
by sense-enjoyments. In these schemes, sense-indul-
gence under certain specified conditions was considered not only harmless but an indispensable desider-

atum. They probably started among some of the Buddhist schools and they soon became very common among certain sects of the Hindus. But the elucidation of these ideas would require a special course of lectures. I shall, therefore, leave them and pass directly to the development of the mysticism of love to God, as it is presented in the Bhagavata Purana and other relevant later literature.   8

It is in the Bhagavata Purana, whose date is probably the eleventh century A. D., that we first meet with the idea of devotion as the supreme source of a bliss or spiritual enjoyment that is itself the highest goal and so completely usurps the place of wisdom or philosophical knowledge. Even in the Gita true wisdom was regarded as a fire which reduces to ashes, as it were, all the past deeds whose fruits were not yet on the point of being enjoyed. But in the Bhagavata we read (11.14) that it is bhakti which destroys all the past sins. The old principle of self-surrender to God and a life spent in God-intoxication is the happiest of all lives. A man of such self-surrender has nothing else but God as his possession: he is supremely self-controlled, and the enjoyment that he has from his constant association with God keeps him absolutely happy and content with all things. Such a man does not aspire to any heavenly happiness or even to liberation. Devotion is regarded as having also a protective virtue. Even an ordinary devotee who is often led away by his sense attachments is so purified by this devotion that he is no longer overcome by external attachments or passions. The Lord can be realized

by bhakti and by nothing else. Neither the performance of the allotted duties nor knowledge combined
with the austere discipline of tapas can purify a man
who is devoid of all bhakti. This bhakti, however, is
no longer the old contemplative meditation of God,
stirred by a deep-seated love. It is the ebullition of
feelings and emotions of attachment to God. It manifests itself in the soft melting of the heart and expresses itself in tears, inarticulate utterances of speech,
laughter, songs and dances, such as can only be possible through a mad intoxication of love. This kind
of bhakti is entirely different from the calm contemplative life of complete self-abnegation and self-surrender to God and a mind wholly immersed in God
and the thought of God.   9

The Bhagavata Purana is aware of the three methods of approach by knowledge, work and devotion,
and also of the approach through yoga. Moreover,
while emphasizing the superiority of devotion, it does
not deny the efficacy of the other methods of approach. The latter are also described in the Gita; indeed, the Gita also emphasizes the bhakti method. Both
the Gita and Bhagavata criticize the older course of
the Vedic sacrifices, but neither of them has the bold-
ness to pass an unconditional condemnation. The Gita
says that one should perform these sacrifices, which
are obligatory, with a pure and desireless mind. The
fault of those who devote themselves to sacrifices is
that they are filled with ordinary desires for pleasures
and are not acquainted with any higher goal of life. To
one who is infused with the higher ideal of life and can

emancipate himself from desires by self-surrender to God, the performance of sacrifices, as of any other kinds of action, can do no harm. Indeed, it is good that under these circumstances one should not forsake his allotted duties.

The Bhagavata holds that the only efficacy of the Vedic restrictions and prohibitions is to be found in the fact that they offer a check on the natural inclinations of man and ultimately help him to desist from sense-activities and sense-propensities. The promise of heavenly rewards as the result of the performance of sacrifices is only a trick to incline people to accommodate themselves to modes of life offering only a restricted scope of sense-gratification. Its appeal is therefore only to those of the lowest plane. Those who are of the next higher order and have been able to accommodate themselves to a life of desirelessness would perform the obligatory duties without in the least looking forward to their fruits. In the next higher stage, a man may follow the path of yoga, or the path of wisdom respecting the supreme unity of Brahman, or any other line of devotion.   10

The path of devotion, however, is most fitted for those who are neither too much attached to sense-desires nor too much detached from them. Such men may adopt the line of bhakti and thereby purify their minds and, by self-surrender to God and the taste of supreme human happiness in their love, become averse to all other desires and enjoyments. Thus they learn to live a life of supreme devotion. They come to experience such intense happiness that all their limbs and senses become saturated therewith and their minds swim, as it were, in a lake of such supreme bliss that even the bliss of ultimate liberation loses its charm. Such an individual desires to live on, enjoying the love of God with heart, soul and body. When he acquires such a bhakti, it purifies his mind from all passions and impurities, and destroys all the bonds of his deeds and their fruits. For such a person is so attached to God that there is nothing else for which he cares; without any effort on his part, other attachments and inclinations lose their hold over him. So great is his passion for God that it consumes all his earthly passions. It is so great that it is its own satisfaction; it seeks nothing beyond itself. It stands by itself. As a great spring of happiness, it is ultimate and self-complete.

The bhakta who is filled with such a passion does not experience it merely as an undercurrent of joy which waters the depths of his heart in his own privacy, but as a torrent that overflows the caverns of his heart into all his senses. Through all his senses he realizes it as if it were a sensuous delight; with his heart and soul he feels it as a spiritual intoxication of joy. Such a person is beside himself with this love of God. He sings, laughs, dances and weeps. He is no longer a person of this world. The germ of this love is already found in the Vishnu Purana, where Prahlada seeks as a boon that bhakti which is an attachment for God no less strong than the attraction to sense-objects felt by ordinary sensual persons. [11]

Vallabha, a later writer, defines bhakti as a great,

firm feeling of love, associated with a sense of God's superiority and greatness. It places the bhakta or the devotee in a subordinate position. The latter is described as approaching God as one approaches his master, desiring mercy and protection and soliciting His special grace. But this idea of seeking protection and special grace, with a sense of God's supreme superiority, and finding oneself happy in thinking of the greatness of the superior Being, is by no means restricted to Hindu circles. There are numerous evidences of Buddhists praising the Buddha and seeking his protection, and finding great joy in extolling his great qualities and powers. Bhaktishataka of Ramachandra Bharati of the 13th century may be referred to as a typical instance.

This kind of bhakti is also associated with the doctrine of prapatti, or taking refuge in God, and is to be found among many classes of Vaishnavas, including the followers of Ramanuja. Prapatti consists in taking refuge in God with great faith and with the strong conviction that it is God and God alone who can help one to attain one's end. Like the fabled bird Chataka that would rather die of thirst than drink any water other than that falling from the clouds, the devotee looks to God for succor, and would seek no other help. Believing that God alone is the saviour, the devotee depends entirely on Him, and refuses to take any other course than that of remaining in entire dependence upon Him. God, for him, is the great master of whom he is the humble servant; God is the controller alike of his mind and his body. **12**

This is only a detailed method of the self-surrender already referred to in the Gita. Naturally the latter also is based on a belief in the great mercy of God, who is sure to free the devotee who with complete reliance has taken refuge in Him as his master and Lord. But in this case the prapatti or taking refuge in God is always with a purpose. It is for the realization of an end that the devotee relies on the mercy, goodness or grace of God. He believes that he can by this means alone attain what he wants. But the bhakti praised in the Bhagavata is of a sort superior to this. It is a devotion without motive of any kind. It is the love of God proceeding directly from the heart and not prompted by any reason. The true bhakta does not love God because he seeks something from Him, but he loves Him freely and spontaneously. He sacrifices everything for this love. It is his only passion in life and he is filled with God. God is attracted by such love and always abides with such a bhakta and encourages his great love for him. All distinctions of caste, creed or social status vanish for those who are filled with this true and sincere devotion to God. It is a great leveller. To the eye of a true bhakta all beings are but manifestations of God's power, and they are all equal. Impelled by this idea of universal equality and by the idea of God being in all things and all things in God, he is filled with such a sweetness of temper that howsoever he may be tyrannized over by any one he cannot think of inflicting any injury in return. Nor can he remain unaffected when

he sees the sufferings of his fellow-beings, however
lowly or depraved they may be.   13

The question is sometimes asked whether such devotional systems of mysticism are pantheistic. To this
no satisfactory reply can be given without a proper
definition of pantheism. Without entering into any
discussion regarding the meaning of this term or the
distinctive metaphysical features of the different systems of Vaishnavism, I can here say only that all these
systems in a manner agree as to the duality of God
and man. They consider man as a manifestation of
the power of God. Though ultimately sustained and
always controlled by God, man is for all empirical
purposes different from Him. This psychological, logical and ontological difference between God and man
is the basis of devotion and worship. In the development of devotion there may, however, come a stage
in the mind of the devotee when he becomes one with
the Lord in the exuberance of his feelings. But at
the next instant the experience may again be differen-
tiated into a feeling of duality and of distinction between him and God. The devotee may then come to
regard himself as a servant of God or His son, or
friend, or spouse. It cannot be said, in this inner
dialectic of feeling, which of the phases is the truer
and has a greater claim to our acceptance. For we
have here an alternation of feeling which sometimes
expresses itself as an experience of communion or
contemplative unity with God and then by its own
inner movement passes for its own realization into
the various other modes of relationships through which

ordinary human love expresses itself. It is a circular movement. At one stage within it, man becomes God, but, at the other, God slowly becomes man and participates with him in diverse human relationships of love and its joys.   14

Love of God is not a thing which we produce in ourselves by excessive brooding or by self-hypnotism or by any other method. It is a permanent flame, slowly burning in the caverns of all our hearts. Only, however, when it gains strength through study, and through association with other devotees at an opportune moment, do we come to know of it. The basis of all religions is this love of God. For if this love of God were not vital to us, all that the great prophets have been trying to preach would have been unreal and futile. If it were not a real experience which in some sense is shared by us all, an experience which ennobles us and raises us far above the selfish pettinesses of life, no prophet and no religious deed would be able to appeal to our higher natures and establish the claims of religion. Religion is by nature an other-worldly attitude of life—one which we have along with our worldly attitude. "Man does not live by bread alone," is a very elastic proposition. If we by nature wanted only that which satisfies our appetites, there would have been no art, no philosophy, and no religion. Our being is such that side by side with the tendencies that take us to the satisfaction of our appetites or to sense-gratifications, there are others which in an unaccountable manner lift us higher. The senses when properly exercised give us sense pleasures; the mind, through its activities of logical thinking, affords the corresponding joys and the satisfaction of truth-seeking; and the spirit longs to associate itself with some higher ideal, with a greater and superior being, or with a transcendent unspeakable something of which it has at first only an indistinct vision.   15

Reason moves within a circle and cannot get beyond it. When the ultimate reason of reasoning is to be sought, we have to rest in a tendency, temperament or feeling. Ask a philosopher why he engages in philosophical speculation. He may say that he seeks to know the truth of some particular or some universal problem. But ask him again why he so seeks and he will probably say that he does it because he finds therein a special satisfaction. The satisfaction, though not measureable in physical terms, is yet enough for him. He possesses intellectual curiosity and it must be gratified. Ask a scientist and you will probably receive the same answer. One can never explain our endeavors in any of the higher planes of life, philosophy, art or religion, by reference to any of the ordinary needs and objects of life. These higher activities are apparently without any reason, but still they justify themselves and they are our very existence. That bread alone should not satisfy man is part of his very nature and there is no getting away therefrom. It is an absolute fact with man. The case of religion is very similar. There is a spiritual longing in the heart of man, indistinct and undefined, but steady like a flame tapering upwards to some divine goal. The mystics of the Bhagavata Purana of whom I am now speaking called it the love of God. They felt that there is nothing higher than the culture of this love. The seed of it they regarded as latent within the individual. Hearing and singing the praises of God stimulates its growth—sprinkles it with water, as it were—until it ascends higher and higher and eventually reaches God. Like an expert gardener the individual has always to see that no beast of a sin, tramples this tender creeper, and that no offshoots, no branches of worldly desires, obstruct its upward growth. Whenever he is tempted by worldly desires or to pray to God for worldly good, he is allowing offshoots to grow on the body of the tender creeper of God's love and to interfere with its upward growth. He must cut them off and make the creeper of love grow freely in one direction, until it connects him with God and he thus comes to enjoy its sweet fruits.   16

The type of bhakti which is preached in the Bhagavata Purana is well illustrated in the life of Chaitanya, who was born in Navadvip, in Bengal, in 1486 and died in 1534. In his life we find an exemplification of how love of God may be cultivated for its own sake, without any kind of ulterior motive whether of liberation or of happiness. In the accounts which his biographers have given of his mysticism, a distinction is drawn between the experience of God's love as self-surrender to Him, or taking refuge in Him through attachment to Him, and a driving passion of love for God, i. e., between what they call *rati* and *preman*. A distinction is also drawn between a course of attachment and love of God adopted out of a sense of duty or of reverence for the scriptures and a passion of love which springs spontaneously and overflows unrestrainedly. A distinction is further made between love of God with an overwhelming sense of His greatness and superiority, awe and reverence, and love of God as an easy flow of affection to one who is nearest and dearest to us. Real intimacy with God is only possible in the case of the latter alternative, when a free flow of passionate love springing spontaneously from within associates us with God as the most intimate friend and beloved without whom we cannot live. Chaitanya acknowledges, of course, the peaceful calm and tender love for God called *shanta,* and the submission of the heart to God in obligation and service to Him, called the service attitude, *dasya;* but to look upon God as one's own most intimate friend, *sakhya,* is regarded by him as higher than either of the first two attitudes. To look upon God as one's dearest beloved or lover, or to love Him with a feminine love as that with which a woman loves her beloved, he considers the deepest, sweetest and most perfect love, *madhura.*

According to the legend, Lord Krishna was born of Devaki and Vasudeva in a prison-house where the King Kansa, who was afraid of the birth of the infant who was foretold to be his future destroyer, had confined his mother Devaki. Later Krishna was carried to the house of a cowherd chief, Nanda. There he grew up, having as his associates cowherd boys with whom he was very friendly. He came to be regarded as God incarnate, as the result of a number

of miracles which he performed. The wives of most
of the cowherd people, who were, in reality but the
female incarnations of God's energy, became attached
to him and loved him dearly. They were sorely pained
over the separation when he later on left for Mathura,
a city at some distance from Brindaban, the scene of
his early activities. Krishna's early life illustrates
the love for him of his fostermother Yashoda, wife
of the cowherd chief Nanda, the love for him of his
cowherd friends, and the love of the cowherd girls for
him as their lover. Inasmuch as Krishna was considered to be God, these three kinds of love for Krishna
as described in the tenth chapter of the Bhagavata
Purana, together with the other two time-honored
modes of loving God, viz., the peaceful quiet love of
God and the love of God as God's servant, came to
be considered as the five fundamental modes of loving
God. The attention of the later Vaishnavas was so
much drawn to the excellence of the three kinds of
love described in the Bhagavata, and particularly of
the love of God as one's lover, that no less than four-
teen commentaries have been published dealing with
this portion of the Bhagavata Purana. Love of
Krishna was the most absorbing passion of Chaitanya's
life and, though he came to taste all the different ways
of loving God, it was the sweet love of Krishna as
the lover, husband and Lord that was the most important feature of his life.   18

Chaitanya's elder brother had turned a recluse. So
his mother Sachi Devi would not at first send Chaitanya to school, since she believed that it is through

knowledge that one learns the transitoriness of all things, and she thought it better that her son should grow untutored than that he become learned and renounce the world. So Chaitanya, or Nimai as he was called in his early life, grew wild. But he gradually grew so wild that he could no longer be tolerated, and so he was sent to school. He mastered Sanskrit grammar and logic very thoroughly and at twenty started a school himself. Numerous anecdotes are told by his biographers of his great scholarship and of occasions when he defeated reputed scholars in open debates. At this period he scoffed at all religions and was considered by many to be absolutely godless. In the meanwhile he had settled down in life. His first wife having died, he married again. But at this time Chaitanya's deeper nature began to reveal itself and he wanted to visit the temple of the God Krishna at Gaya, several hundred miles distant from his village. On his way thither he met a great Vaishnava saint and at his sight his higher spiritual life was stirred into life. When he reached the temple of Gaya he experienced a rapturous fervor of love for Krishna, and he became an entirely different man. "Where is my God Krishna," became his chief cry. In thinking of Krishna, in seeking Him, in relating his vision of Him, he would be so overpowered as often to become unconscious. It was in this condition that he was brought home from Gaya by his friends. He spent his days and nights in reciting and singing the name of God. He, his intimate friend Nityananda, and his other friends used thus to sing the name of God and to dance about with a particular type of music produced by special musical instruments. This music touched the inner, spiritual chords of life and brought on a great religious intoxication in all the hearers, and particularly in Chaitanya and his followers. Chaitanya lived continually in this state of religious intoxication. He had no respect for caste or creeds but was a friend of all. He could not continue this sort of life midst the worldly conditions of his native village. Hence he renounced the world to preach the love of God all over India. In this work he spent the rest of his years, going about from place to place, thousands of miles, on foot. The vision of God was always before him in the form of Lord Krishna. His whole life was a passionate flow of love for this deity, and this emotion was generally so intense that as he sang and danced like a mad man he often became unconscious. He had so thoroughly identified himself as a partner in the episodes of the life of Krishna as described in the Bhagavata that the slightest incidents deriving either from personal conversations and relations or from the scenes of nature sufficed to suggest to him similar adventures or events in the life of Krishna.   19

Chaitanya described God's love in its most exalted form as being like the love of a woman in deep attachment to a man, where the attachment is so deep that all sex considerations have ceased—a love so intense that only an insatiable desire of union in love remains and all the earthly relations of man and woman have ceased. God, he taught, is himself a great controller of us all, and in His eternal love is always attracting us, drawing us up toward greater and greater perfection. Love is His very nature. So it is only through a passionate love of Him that we can enjoy His deep love for us. The older ideals of liberation, of heavenly happiness, of the destruction of the mind and the like were considered by Chaitanya to be absolutely insignificant for a person whose mind has been fired by a great passion that flows in torrents to God, the great ocean of love, who washes away all his sins and defects. In the end, Chaitanya, in an outbreak of divine passion which he was unable to restrain, jumped into the deep blue ocean on the South and was lost forever to human eyes. So passed away one drop of God's love in human shape into that eternal and limitless Ocean of divine love from which it had descended upon the earth. 20

LECTURE VI
POPULAR DEVOTIONAL MYSTICISM

LECTURE VI
POPULAR DEVOTIONAL MYSTICISM

THE chief features of the passionate devotion for God described in the last lecture are its spontaneity and its transference of human relations and emotions to God through the medium of the Krishna legend described in the Bhagavata Purana. It presupposes the theory of the incarnation of God as man, which makes it possible to think of God in human relations and in human ways. The idea of God as father is indeed as old as the Vedas. It is expressed also in several passages of the Gita (9.17, 11.43, 11.44, 14.4) and in the Puranas, in the Nyaya-bhashya of Vatsyayana, as well as elsewhere. Nevertheless it did not, during this period, seem to gain much strength in the way of fostering an intimate relation with God or of affecting worship. Wherever it appears it seems to be but one of the many passing phases in which God's relation to man is viewed when God is praised and extolled in His greatness as Lord and Master. But in the new school of bhakti the conception of God as creator, supporter, father, lord and master, or as the ultimate philosophical principle, is subordinated to the conception of god as the nearest and dearest. The most important feature is His nearness to and His intimacy with us—not His great powers, which create a distance between Him and us. That He is the greatest of the great and the Highest of the high, that there is nothing greater and higher than Him is admitted by all. His greatness, however, does not reveal the secret of why He should be so dear to us. He may be the greatest, highest, loftiest and the most transcendent, but yet He has made His home in our hearts and has come down to our level to give us His affection and love. Indeed He is conceived as so near to us that we can look upon Him and love Him with the love of a very dear friend, or with the devotion and the intensity of love of a spouse. Love is a great leveller; the best way of realizing God is by making Him an equal partner in life by the force of intense love.   1

The legend of Krishna supplies a human touch to God's dealings with men. With the help of this legend the bhaktas of the new school, by a peculiar mystical turn of mind, could conceive of God as at once a great being with transcendent powers and also as an intimate friend or a dear lover maintaining human relations with his bhaktas. The episodes of Krishna's life in Brindaban are spiritualized. They are often conceived to happen on a non-physical plane where both Krishna and his partners are thought to play their parts of love and friendship in non-physical bodies. Thus they are not regarded as particular events that took place at specific points of time in the life of a particular man, Krishna. They are interpreted as the eternal, timeless and spaceless play of God with His own associates and His energies, with whom He eternally realizes Himself in love and friendship. The

part that his bhaktas had to play was to identify themselves, by a great stretch of sympathy, as partners in
or spectators of God's love-play, and find their fullest
satisfaction in the satisfaction of God. For a true
bhakta, it is not necessary, therefore, that his sense-
inclinations should be destroyed. What is necessary
is merely that these should be turned towards God and
not towards himself, i. e., that he use his senses not
for his own worldly satisfaction but to find enjoyment
and satisfaction in the great love-drama of God by
identifying himself with one of the spiritual partners of God in his love-play. Hence it is not essential
that all desires and sense-functions, as the Gita says,
be destroyed, or that the individual behave as if he had
desires while yet being absolutely desireless. It was
required that the bhakta have the fullest satisfaction
of his sense and inclinations by participating in the
joys of Krishna in his divine love-play. For such
participation and vicarious enjoyment was regarded
as true love (*preman*), while the satisfaction of one's
own senses or of one's own worldly purposes was
viewed as a vicious passion. Thus here we have a
new scheme of life. The ideal of desirelessness and
absolute self-control is replaced by that of participation in a drama of divine joy, and the desires are given
full play in the direction of God. Desires are not to
be distinguished; only their directions are to be
changed. 2

Though this form of bhakti has in various circles
at times been debased and encroached upon by diverse
kinds of eroticism or erotic mysticism, it cannot be

denied that many of the immediate and later followers of Chaitanya achieved great spiritual success in
this form of bhakti-worship.　In the Narayaniya chapter of the fifth canto of the Mahabharata God is spoken
of as a father, mother and teacher; and in the Yoga
Sutra of Patanjali and elsewhere the idea is often
expressed that God originally taught the Vedas to the
sages and that He is therefore the original teacher.
In all these writings, however, the love of God super-
cedes deep reverence.　The true bhakta looked upon
God as the divine dispenser; he considered all that he
had—kingdoms, riches, wife and all that he could call
his own—to be God's.　Love of God as the mother of
the world plays an important part in the religious attitude of many bhakti worshippers. This is particularly
true in the case of Ramprasad and others, notably the
sage Ramakrishna of recent times.　And in this at-
tribution of motherliness to God both Ramprasad and
Ramakrishna view Him as a tender mother who is always helping her child, condoning his sins and trans-
gressions, partial to his weaknesses and concerned to
better him.　Nevertheless He cannot be attained by
mere formal worship but only through a whole-hearted
worship, with a proper control of the sense-inclina-
tions.　　　　　　　　　　　　　　　　　　　　　　3

The theory of bhakti seems to have its original
source in the Pancaratra school of Vaishnavism.
However, the doctrine of supreme self-surrender to
Narayana, Hari or Krishna as the one and only God
in disregard of all other mythical gods, represents a
teaching of the Gita, the chief work of the Ekanti

school of Vaishnavas; and this doctrine forms the universal basis of all kinds of bhakti worship, though among the Shaktas or Shaivas the supreme deity went by the name of Shakti or Shiva. The Gita plainly teaches, as we have already pointed out in our previous lecture, that there is no other God but Narayana or Krishna, that He alone is great and that we should lay aside all other modes of religious worship and take refuge in Him. In Chaitanya this devotion to God developed into a life-absorbing passion; yet in all advanced forms of bhakti the chief emphasis is on supreme attachment to God. The sort of bhakti which Prahlada asked as a boon from Hari was such an attachment for Him as worldly persons have for the objects of their senses. Such a bhakti, as described in the Bhagavata or the Shandilya sutra, is not worship out of a sense of duty or mere meditation on God or mere singing of His name, but it is deep affection (*anurakti*). It is therefore neither knowledge nor any kind of activity, but is a feeling. And the taking of refuge (*prapatti*) in God is also not motivated by knowledge but by a deep affection which impels the individual to take his first and last stay in Him. But though a feeling, this bhakti does not bind anyone to the world. For the world is but a manifestation of God's maya, and God so arranges for those who love Him that His maya cannot bind His bhakta to the world.   4

But how is such a bhakti possible? For this also we have ultimately to depend on God. There is a passage in the Upanishads (Katha II. 23) which states that He can be attained by him whom He (God) chooses. This text has often been cited to indicate that it is only the chosen man of God who has the privilege of possessing a special affection for God. Vallabha declares this special favor (*pushti*) of God indispensable for the rise of such an affection for God. He further holds that according to the different degrees of the favor of God one may have different degrees of affection for Him, though by avoiding the commission of sinful actions, by cleansing the mind of the impurities of worldly passions, and by inclining the mind towards God, one may go a great way in deserving His special favor. It is only by the highest special favor of God that one's affection or attachment for Him can become an all-consuming and all-engulfing passion (*vyasana*—see the Prameyaratnarnava). True devotion to God, affection or love for Him, must always be an end in itself and never a means to any other end, not even salvation or liberation, so much praised in the classical systems of philosophy. This all-absorbing passion for God is the bhakta's eternal stay in God, and dearer to him than liberation or any other goal of religious realization.   5

It is not out of place here to mention that among various Hindu sects it was held that an engrossing passion of any kind may so possess the whole mind that all other mental functions may temporarily be suspended, and that gradually, through the repeated occurrence of such a passion, the other mental functions may be altogether annihilated. Thus, absorption in a single supreme passion may make the mind so one-pointed that all other attachments are transcended and the individual attains Brahmahood (see the Spandapradipika). In the Upanishads (Brihadaranyaka IV. 3.21) we find that the bliss of Brahman is compared with the loving embrace of a beloved woman. To love one's husband and to serve him as a god was regarded from very early times as the only spiritualizing duty for a woman. Hence the idea that ordinary man-and-woman love may be so perfected as to become a spiritual force easily won acceptance in certain circles. This man-and-woman love developed an absorbing and dominant passion, completely independent and unaided by other considerations of marital and parental duties. In its non-marital forms, it was considered to be capable of becoming so deep as to become by itself a spiritualizing force. Moreover, it was thought that the transition from human love to divine love was so easy that a man who had specialized in the experience of deep man-and-woman love of a non-marital type could easily change the direction of his love from woman to God, and thus indulge in a passionate love for God. The story is told that in his early career the saint Bilvamangala became so deeply attached to a courtesan named Cintamani that one night he swam across a river supported by a floating corpse, then scaled a high wall by holding on to the tail of a serpent, and finally well-nigh broke his limbs in jumping down from the wall into the yard of Cintamani. The woman, however, rebuked him, saying that if he entertained toward God a little of the love that he had for her he would be a saint. This produced such a wonderful change in Bilvamangala that he forthwith became a God-intoxicated man. Later, in his saintly life, when he once again felt attracted by a woman, he plucked out his eyes so that external forms and colors might not further tempt him. This blind saint became one of the best-reputed among all the saints, devoting his life to the love of God.   6

Thus there grew up a school of mystics, including the great poet Candidas and others, who devoted themselves to the cultivation of the spirituality of love and the deification of human love, and who thought that more could be learned through such efforts than through any other mode of worship. "There is no god or goddess in Heaven who can teach spiritual truths more than the person whom one loves with the whole heart." The goddess Basuli whom Candidas worshipped is said to have admonished him to adhere to his love for the washerwoman Rami, saying that Rami would be able to teach him truths that no one else could, and to lead him to such bliss as not even the creator himself might do. A somewhat similar idea of the purificatory power of intense human love is found in the Vishnupurana. In describing the illicit love of a cowherd-girl for Krishna, the Vishnupurana says that at her separation from him she underwent so much suffering that all her sins were expiated, and that in thinking of him in her separation from him she had so much delight as would be equal to the collective culmination of all the happiness that she could enjoy as a reward of her virtuous actions. By the combination of the suffering and the bliss, she exhausted all the fruits of her bad and good deeds, and thus by her thoughts of Krishna she attained her liberation. Somewhat allied with the idea of human worship, though not of the man-and-women type just mentioned, is a certain attitude sometimes adopted toward man as a religious teacher. The latter was considered in many circles as the representative of God on earth, and self-surrender, love and devotion to him was considered to lead one to God. This sort of worship was prevalent among the Hindus and the Buddhists from pretty early times. One fact should be noted. It was associated with reverence and a sense of the religious teacher's superiority, whereas the other type of worship (through romantic love) raised the man and woman by their constancy and sufferings for each other and the happiness that each enjoys in the company and thought of the other. In this latter case, love is religion, and all pain endured for the beloved, joy. With the exception of the phase of love-mysticism just mentioned, I have thus far confined myself to a description of different forms of mysticism as portrayed in Sanskrit writings. I shall now turn to the mysticism of divine love that found expression in the vernaculars of North India and of the South. But this is a vast subject and I can say only a few words. 7

Let me advert first to the Alvar saints of the South, the earliest of whom belonged to the second and the latest to the tenth century, A. D. They all wrote psalms or songs in Tamil, a Dravidian tongue of South India. They were inspired by the teachings of Vaishnavism when it travelled from the North to the South.

Their doctrines were more or less similar to those touched upon in the preceding lecture in connection with the bhakti mysticism of the Bhagavata Purana and the Gita. They are embodied in psalms and not in any connected philosophical treatise. Describing his insatiable love of God, Nam Alvar says:

> "As I dote on the Lord of Katkarai (God)
> Whose streets with scarlet lily are perfumed
> My heart for his wonderful graces melts
> How then can I, my restless love suppress?"[1]

With reference to Nam Alvar, Govindacarya has said: "Briefly, Saint Nam Alvar declares that when one is overcome by bhakti exaltation, trembling in every cell of his being, he must freely and passively allow this influence to penetrate his being, and carry him beyond all known states of consciousness; never from fear or shame that bystanders may take him for a madman, ought the exhibition of this bhakti-rapture that deluges his being, to be suppressed. The very madness is the means of distinguishing him from the ordinary mortals to whom such beatific vision is necessarily denied. The very madness is the bhakta's pride. In that very madness, the saint exhorts, "run, jump, cry, laugh and sing, and let every man witness it."   8

Let us now pass on to other saints of the South, Namdev and Tukaram. The bhakti school referred to in the last lecture, and most of the other branches of this school, developed under purely Brahminic traditions and in the shadow of Brahminic scriptures,

---

[1] Govindacarya's translation.

the Puranas and the like. And though in the Bhagavata we find that even the foreign and aboriginal races
of the Kiratas, Hunas, Andhras, Pulindas, Pukkasas,
Abhiras, Suhmas, Yavanas, Khasas, etc., become pure
if they are attached to God, yet the Brahminic civilization had such a hold over the country that the cult of
bhakti grew up around the traditional cult of Rama,
or Krishna, Shiva or Shakti. Representation of God
in images and their worship by the bhaktas, faith in
the legends of Krishna and other inferior deities as
told in the Puranas, preferential treatment of the
Brahmin caste, respect to the Vedas, etc., became very
intimately associated with the doctrine of bhakti
preached in the Puranas and other Sanskrit scriptures.
We know, of course, that the bhakti cult spread also
among foreigners. Thus, in the second century B. C.,
the Greek king Heliodorus, son of Dios, dedicated to
Vasudeva a flagstaff bearing an image of the bird Ga-
ruda, on which the God Vasudeva or Krishna was said
to ride. Now, though the sons of some demons are
also known to have been great bhaktas, as described
in the Puranas, yet the latter all accepted the traditional God Vasudeva and they regarded the legends
associated with Krishna or Vasudeva as real episodes
of his life. In the thirteenth century A. D., we find
that Visoba Khecar, the teacher of the bhakta Namdev, denounced the worship of images as a substitute for the God Krishna or for any other god. He is
said to have instructed Namdev to abandon image-
worship, saying: "A stone god never speaks. What
possibility then of his removing the disease of mun-

dane existence? A stone image is regarded as God,
but the true God is wholly different. If a stone god
fulfills desires, how is it he breaks when struck? Those
who adore a god made of stone, lose everything
through their folly. Those who say and hear that a
god of stone speaks to his devotees are both of them
fools. Whether a holy place is small or large there
is no god but stone or water. There is no place which
is devoid of God. That God has shown Nama in his
heart and thus Khecar conferred a blessing on him."[2]
Namdev was a tailor by caste and he worshipped the
idol at Pandharpur in the Maratha country in South
India. However, he had a full knowledge of the true
nature of God, as had other bhaktas of Sanskritic traditions. Thus he says: "The Veda has to speak by
Thy might and the Sun has to move round; such is the
might of Thee, the Lord of the Universe. Knowing
this essential truth I have surrendered myself to Thee.
By Thy might it is that the clouds have to pour down
rain, mountains to rest firm and the wind to blow."[3]
Again: "Vows, fasts and austerities are not at all
necessary; nor is it necessary for you to go on a pil-
grimage. Be you watchful in your hearts and always
sing the name of Hari. It is not necessary to give up
eating food or drinking water; fix your mind on the
foot of Hari. Neither is it necessary for you to con-
template the one without attributes. Hold fast to the
love of the name of Hari." "Recognize him alone to
be a righteous man, who sees Vasudeva in all objects,

---

[2] Bhandarkar's *Vaishnavism.*
[3] *Ibid.*

eradicating all pride or egoism. The rest are entangled in the shackles of delusion. To him all wealth is like earth, and the nine gems are mere stones. The two, desire and anger, he has thrown out, and he cherishes in his heart quietude and forgiveness."[4] Again he says: "Firmly grasp the truth which is Narayana. Purity of conduct should not be abandoned; one should not be afraid of the censure of people and thus accomplish one's own purpose. Surrender yourself to your loving friend (God) giving up all ostentation and pride. The censure of people should be regarded as praise and their praise not heeded. One should entertain no longing for being respected and honored, but should nourish in oneself a liking for devotion. This should be rendered firm in the mind and the name of God should not be neglected even for a moment."[5]   9

The essence of the teachings of Namdev, as of almost all the other bhaktas of whom I shall now be speaking, is purity of mind, speech, and deed, utter disregard of castes, creeds and other social distinctions, a tendency to leave all for God, and in love and joy to live in God always, utterly ignoring all social, communal and religious prejudices, narrowness, dogmas and bigotry. It is held that God is omnipotent and omnipresent and that He cannot be identified with any particular deity or his character properly narrated by any particular legendary or mythical ways of thinking. At the same time it is contended

---

[4] *Ibid.*

[5] *Ibid.*

that we may call him by any name we like, for He is
always the same in all.   10

Another great Maratha saint was Tukaram of the
seventeenth century. Tukaram was a low class Hindu.
His father was a petty trader. When his father, in
his old age, wanted to give over his business to his
eldest son Savji, the latter refused the task since he
did not wish a worldly life. So the business was en-
trusted to Tukaram when he was at the age of thir-
teen. Four years later his father died. Then Tukaram
was imposed upon by crafty persons and his business
was wrecked. His wife, however, procured a loan;
the business was restored and then he began to prosper.
Once, however, while he was returning home, Tukaram
met a man who was on the point of being dragged to
prison for his debts. Tukaram at once gave all that
he had to this debtor in order to achieve his release.
From that time on Tukaram renounced all worldly
vocations and devoted his life to singing the glories
of God and the dearness of our relations to Him. He
employed a particular kind of verse which he often
composed extempore and in which he frequently spoke.
Thus Tukaram says: "God is ours, certainly ours,
and is the soul of all souls. God is near to us, certainly near, outside and inside. God is benignant, certainly benignant, and fulfills every longing even of a
longing nature." Again he says: "This thy nature
is beyond the grasp of the mind or of words, and
therefore I have made devoted love a measure. I
measure the endless by the measure of love. He is
not to be truly measured by any other means. Thou

art not to be found by processes of concentration, sacrificial rites, practice of austerities, or any bodily exertions, or by knowledge. Oh Kesava, accept the service which we render to thee in the simplicity of our hearts." Still again: "The Endless is beyond, and between him and me there are lofty mountains of desire and anger. I am not able to ascend them, nor do I find any pass. Insurmountable is the ascent of my enemies. What possibility is there of my attaining my friend Narayana (God)?" He expresses his heart full of longing for God in the following words:[6]

"As on the bank the poor fish lies
And gasps and writhes in pain,
Or, as a man with anxious eyes
Seeks hidden gold in vain,—
So is my heart distressed and cries
To come to thee again.
    Thou knowest, Lord, the agony
    Of the lost infant's wail
    Yearning his mother's face to see.
        (How oft I tell this tale.)
    O, at thy feet the mystery
    Of the dark world unveil.
The fire of this harassing thought
Upon my bosom prays.
Why is it I am thus forgot?
(O, who can know thy ways?)
Nay, Lord, thou seest my hapless lot;
Have mercy, Tuka says."

Desolate and disconsolate for the love of God he prays at His door:

---

[6] This and the immediately following translations are taken from Macnicol's work, *Psalms of the Maratha Saints.*

"A beggar at thy door,
Pleading I stand;
Give me an alms, O God,
Love from thy loving hand.
        Spare me the barren task,
        To come, and to come for nought.
        A gift poor Tuka craves,
        Unmerited, unbought."

Again:

"O save me, save me, Mightiest,
Save me and set me free.
O let the love that fills my breast
Cling to thee lovingly.
        Grant me to taste how sweet thou art;
        Grant me but this, I pray,
        And never shall my love depart
        Or turn from thee away.
Then I thy name shall magnify
And tell thy praise abroad,
For very love and gladness I
Shall dance before my God.
        Grant to me, Vitthal, that I rest
        Thy blessed feet beside;
        Ah, give me this, the dearest, best,
        And I am satisfied."   11

Leaving this bhakti movement of the South, which
dates from the thirteenth to the seventeenth century,
from Jnanesvar and Namdev to Tukaram, we pass to
the bhakti movement of North India, represented by
Kabir, Nanak and others. It followed the line traced
by the Gita and the Bhagavata. Having been developed
in the vernacular, however, it appealed directly to the
masses. It largely dissociated itself from the complex
entanglements of Hindu mythology which had en-

meshed the devotional creed of spiritual loyalty to God in the legend of Krishna and his associates.   12

Kabir (1440-1518) was an abandoned child, probably because of the illegitimacy of his birth. He was brought up by a weaver, Niru, and his wife, Nina. Throughout his life he lived in Benares, probably himself following the profession of a weaver. He is said to have been a disciple of Ramananda, a disciple of Ramanuja, the great Vaishnava teacher of the South. But he likewise came into touch with some Mohammedan Pirs and was also probably acquainted with certain forms of Sufism. His was a religion which derived its life from what was best among both the Hindus and the Mohammedans. However, he disliked the bigotry and superstitions of all formal religions and was consequently persecuted by both the Hindus and the Mohammedans. With him and his followers, such as Ruidas and Dadu, we find a religion which shook off all the traditional limitations of formal religions, with their belief in revealed books and their acceptance of mythological stories, and of dogmas and creeds that often obscure the purity of the religious light and contact with God. Kabir considered the practice of yoga, alms, and fasting, and the feeding of Brahmins, not only useless but improper without the repetition of God's name and love for Him. He discarded the Hindu ideas regarding purity, external ablutions and contact with so-called impure things with as much force as he rejected the Mohammedan belief in circumcision or the requirement that a Brahmin should wear a holy thread, or any other marks of caste. When

Kabir's parents found that they could not subdue his Hindu tendencies they wanted to circumcise him, and at this he said:

"Whence have come the Hindus and Mussulmans? Who hath
    put them in their different ways,
Having thought and reflected in thy heart, answer this—who
    shall obtain Heaven and who Hell."[7]   13

Now we know that the doctrine of bhakti had a great levelling influence. Even according to the Gita and the Bhagavata Purana, bhakti removed all inequalities of caste and social status. We know that Haridas (his Mohammedan name is not known) was converted from Mohammedanism to Vaishnavism by Chaitanya and Nityananda. In lauding him Chaitanya once said: "Your holy thoughts are as the streams of the Ganges in which your soul bathes every hour. Your pious acts earn for you that virtue which the people seek in sacrificial rites prescribed in the scriptures. You are constantly in touch with the loftiest of ideals which give you the same merit as the study of the Vedas. What sadhu or Brahmin is there who is good and great as you are?"[8] In the Brihat Naradiya Purana we find that even a candala (the lowest caste among the Hindus) becomes the greatest of all Brahmins if he loves God. So the new religious ideal of bhakti, in all its enthusiastic circles, dispensed with

---

[7] Most of the translations of Kabir's hymns are from the translation of *The Bijak of Kabir* by the Rev. Ahmed Shah. There are some which I translated directly from the hymns in Hindu.

[8] Sen's *Chaitanya and his Companions*, p. 69.

the considerations of caste, creed, and social status. 14

There was, therefore, nothing particularly novel in Kabir's insistence that the time-honored distinctions of caste, creed and social status are absolutely value-less or in his emphasis upon the need of bhakti for all, as that which alone exalts a man. But in Kabir we find a reformatory zeal. He never tires of reiterating the worthlessness of all these superstitions of caste, creed, social status, external purity and impurity, penances, asceticism, and all sorts of formalities which passed by the name of religion though in fact having nothing to do with it. Thus Kabir says:

"If union with God be obtained by going about naked,
 All the deer of the forest shall be saved.
 What mattereth it whether man goeth naked or weareth a
   deerskin,
 If he recognize not God in his heart?
 If perfection be obtained by shaving the head,
 Why should not sheep obtain salvation?
 If, O brethren, the continent man is saved,
 Why should not a eunuch obtain the supreme reward?
 Saith Kabir, hear, O my brethren,
 Who hath obtained salvation without God's name?"

Again he says:

"They who battle in the evening and the morning
 Are like frogs in the water.
 When men have no love for God's name,
 They shall all go to the god of death.
 They who love their persons and deck themselves out in
   various guises,
 Feel not mercy even in their dreams.
 Many leading religious men call them quadrupeds,
 And say that only holy men shall obtain happiness in this
   ocean of trouble.

Saith Kabir, why perform so many ceremonies?
Forsaking all other essences quaff the great essence
of God's name."

These allusions to bathing and other activities refer
to religious practices followed by many Hindus but
vigorously denounced by Kabir.   15

To a Yogin who said to Kabir that one could not attain deliverance without chastening his heart by the
performance of yoga Kabir said:

"Without devotion the qualities of the heart cling to the heart,
Who secured perfection by merely chastening his heart?
What holy man has succeeded in chastening his heart?
Say who hath saved any one by merely chastening his heart.
Every one thinketh in his heart that he is going to chasten it,
But the heart is not chastened without devotion.
Saith Kabir, let him who knoweth this secret
Worship in his heart God, the lord of the three worlds."

Kabir in speaking of the search after God says:

"When I turned my thoughts toward God, I restrained my mind
    and my senses, and my attention became lovingly fixed on Him.
O Bairagi, search for Him who neither cometh nor goeth, who
    neither dieth nor is.
My soul turning away from sin, is absorbed in the universal
    soul."

Describing the view that God is not confined to any
mosque, church or temple, Kabir says:

"If God dwell only in the mosque, to whom belongeth the
    rest of the country?
They who are called Hindus say that God dwelleth in
    an idol:
          I see not the truth in either sect.
O God, whether Allah or Ram, I live by Thy name,
O Lord, show kindness unto me.

Hari dwelleth in the south, Allah hath his place in the
west.
Search in thy heart, search in thy heart of hearts; there
is his place and abode.
The Brahmins yearly perform twenty-four fastings . . .
the Mussulmans fast in the month of Ramzan.
. . . Kabir is a child of Ram and Allah and accepteth
all gurus and Pirs."

Describing his great love and intoxication for God,
Kabir says:

"I am not skilled in book knowledge, nor do I understand
controversy:
I have grown mad reciting and hearing God's praises.
O father, I am mad; the whole world is sane; I am mad;
I am ruined; let not others be ruined likewise;
I have not grown mad out of my own will; God hath
made me mad—
The true guru hath dispelled my doubts—
I am ruined, and have lost my intellect;
Let nobody be led astray in doubts like mine.
He who knoweth not himself is mad;
When one knoweth himself he knoweth the one God.
He who is not intoxicated with divine love in this human
birth shall never be so.
Saith Kabir, I am dyed with the dye of God."

Thus, on the one hand, Kabir waged war against
the prevailing superstitions, rituals and litanies of all
religions and religious sects; and, on the other hand,
he dived deep in the depth of God's love and he be-
held nothing but God on all sides, becoming as it were
one with Him in spiritual union. Thus, he says:

"With both mine eyes I look,
But I behold nothing save God;
Mine eyes gaze affectionately on Him."

The motto of his life was, as he often said, "Remember God, Remember God, Remember God, my brethren;" and in his own life he felt that he was absorbed in the Infinite.   16

Rui Das (also called Ravi Das), a shoe-maker by caste, was another great disciple of Ramananda. His songs and hymns are full of humility and devotion. However, he evidences none of the reformatory zeal that animated Kabir. I shall quote the translation of only one hymn which seems to me typical of Rui Das's attitude of love towards God. He says:

> "There is none so poor as I, none so compassionate as
>   Thou;
> For this what further test is now necessary?
> May my heart obey thy words, fill thy servant therewith.
> I am a sacrifice to thee, O God;
> Why art thou silent?
> For many births have I been separated from Thee, O
>   God;
> This birth is on thine own account.
> Saith Rui Das, putting my hopes in Thee, I live; it is
>   long since I have seen thee."   17

Still another great saint of love was Mira Bai, a princess of Rajputana, who from her childhood (born about 1504 A. D.) was devoted to an image of Lord Krishna called Girdharlal. Her marriage proved unhappy. At the time of going to her husband's place she became very disconsolate. She wept until she became unconscious at the idea of leaving the image of Girdharlal behind. So her parents gave her the image as a part of her marriage dowry. It proved that Mira could not get on well with the family of her father-in-law, for she was always given to the adoration and worship of her little image, representing to her Lord Krishna, and it was this image that she considered as her husband. Her father-in-law made attempts to kill her, but she was miraculously saved. Ultimately she left his abode and went to Brindaban, the place of Lord Krishna's activities, to have her passion for Krishna realized. Here again, in the case of this princess saint who left her all for Krishna, we find the potency of the Krishna legend.   18

I shall quote here the translation of one of Mira Bai's hymns which show her great attachment for Krishna, in an image of whom, at Dvaraka, she was, as the tradition says, ultimately lost. Her soul was so full of deep longing for Lord Krishna, or Girdhar as she called him, that she proclaims:

"I have the god Girdhar and no other;
   He is my spouse on whose head is a crown of peacock
      feathers,
   Who carrieth a shell, discus, mace and lotus, and who
      weareth a necklace;
   I have forfeited the respect of the world by ever sit-
      ting near holy men.
The matter is now public; everybody knoweth it.
Having felt supreme devotion I die as I behold the world.
I have no father, son, or relation with me.
I laugh when I behold my beloved; people think I weep.
I have planted the vine of love and irrigated it again
      and again with the water of tears,
I have cast away my fear of the world, what can any-
      one do to me
Mira's love for her god is fixed, come what may."   19

India is a land of saints. There are hundreds of

them of whom one could say much. But my time is limited and I have well-nigh exhausted your patience. Yet I cannot conclude without referring briefly to Tulsidas, the greatest Hindu poet of India and a great saint.

Tulsidas lived in the seventeenth century. He did not inaugurate any new faith, but accepted the Hindu mythology and the theory of the incarnation of God, the appearance of the attributeless God as a God of infinite attributes. In his view Rama was the incarnation of God, the savior and father of mankind. An all-surrendering devotion to him, he believed, is our only duty and the sole legitimate passion of life. God is great not only in His greatness, but also in his mercy. He knows the sins and the frailties of men, and is always prepared to help them repel their temptations. To run counter to the will of God is sin, and it is only by acknowledging our sins and taking an all-surrendering refuge in Him, in love and faith, that we can be saved. Connected herewith was the doctrine of the brotherhood of man and of our duty toward our neighbors. Tulsidas is said to have been very much attached to his wife in his early life. On one occasion he followed her to her father's place, much to her annoyance, and she said that if he had as much love for God Rama as he had for her he would be saved. This struck Tulsidas to the heart and he renounced the world. By his great strength of character, his remarkable poetic gifts which he applied to religious subjects, and by his strong faith, Tulsidas soon endeared himself to his countrymen. No one has exercised a greater influence than he over the Hindi-speaking people of North India.   20

I have now described, though but briefly, some of the main types of Indian mysticism in their mutual relations; others could not be so much as touched upon owing to the limitations of time. I am fully alive to the imperfections of my treatment. Great as they are, they must have appeared to you even greater on account of the difficulty that you must have experienced in placing yourselves on the mental plane of these mystics. The subtle metaphysical and philosophical background of these different types of mysticism I have here been compelled to disregard. But I have elsewhere undertaken an historical survey of all the different systems of Indian Philosophy.[9] Through oral instruction, tradition, and the example of great men who renounced the world in pursuance of the high ideals of philosophy, the essence of these different systems, with their spiritual longings and their yearnings after salvation and the cessation of rebirth, have gradually been filtering down into the minds of the masses of the population. The tiller of the soil and the grocer in the shop may be uneducated and often wholly illiterate, but even they, while tilling the ground, driving a bullock cart or resting after the work of the day, will be singing songs full of mystical meaning, and for the moment transporting themselves

---

[9] In my *History of Indian Philosophy,* the first volume of which has already been published by the Cambridge University Press, England.

to regions beyond the touch of material gains and comforts:

"The sky and the earth are born of mine own eyes.
The hardness and softness, the cold and the heat are
    the products of my own body;
The sweet smell and the bad are of my own nose."

Or,

"Nobody can tell whence the bird unknown
Comes into the cage and goes out.
I would feign put round its feet the fetter of my mind
Could I but capture it."[10]

A traveller in the village of Bengal or on board the steamers plying the rivers of the interior of rural Bengal, may often hear a middle-aged or old Mohammedan or a Hindu singing mystical, philosophical or mythical songs of the love of Krishna and Radha, or of the renouncement of the world by Chaitanya, while a large crowd of men is assembled around the singer listening to him with great reverence and feeling. The singer is probably describing the world as a mirage or a mere phantom show of *maya,* or is expressing the futility of his worldly life on account of his having lost his friendship with his own self.

"My hope of the world is all false,
    What shall be my fate,
        O kind, good lord?
I am not in love with him (self) with whom
    I have come to live in this house (body)
        O kind, good lord."

---

[10] Dr. Rabindranath Tagore's opening address at the First Philosophical Congress at Calcutta, in 1925.

So the sublime teachings of philosophy and the other-worldly aspirations of mysticism, with their soothing, plaintive and meditative tendencies, have watered the hearts of Bengal right into the thatched cottages of this land. Wealth and comfort they all appreciate as do people everywhere, but they all know that money is not everything, and that peace of mind and the ultimate good of man cannot be secured through it or any other worldly thing. They are immersed in the world; but still the wisdom of the ages and the teachings of the saints have not been in vain, and at times they are drawn away from the world— their souls unknowingly long for deliverance and find a mystic delight in it. It is only the educated or Anglicized Hindu who, dazzled by the gay colors of the West, sometimes turns a deaf ear to the old tune of his country—the flute of Krishna calling from afar through the rustling leaves of bamboos and the cocoanut groves of the village homes—and, in the name of patriotism and progress, installs a foreign god of money and luxury in the ancestral throne of the god of the Indian heart—the god of deliverance. The thoughts and aspirations of the ages, our myths, our religions, our philosophies, our songs and poetry, have all interpenetrated and formed a whole which cannot be expressed through a portrayal of its elements. They represent a unique experience which I feel with my countrymen, but which is incommunicable to any one who is unable imaginatively to bring himself into tune with that spirit. The British in India have understood as much of the country as is necessary for policing it, but no foreigner has ever adequately understood our land. Those of you who see India through newspapers and the strange tales and stories of tourists who "do" India in a month, can hardly hope to go right to the place where the heart of India lies.   21

But, you may perhaps ask, what may I gain by knowing India as it really is at its heart? Well, that is a different matter. Perhaps you may derive gain, perhaps not. You may further ask what is it that one gains through such spiritual longing, realization, or mystical rapture. And I shall frankly confess that one certainly gains nothing that will show itself in one's bank account. But with all my appreciation and admiration of the great achievements of the West in science, politics and wealth, the Upanishad spirit in me may whisper from within: What have you gained if you have not gained yourself, the immortal, the infinite? What have you gained if you have never tasted in your life the deep longing for deliverance and supreme emancipation? And the spirit of the saints of ages whispers in my ears: What have you gained if you have not tasted the joys of self-surrender, if your heart has not longed to make of you a flute in the hands of Krishna, that master musician of the universe, and if you have not been able to sweeten all your miseries with a touch of God?   22

CPSIA information can be obtained
at www.ICGtesting.com
Printed in the USA
LVHW01s2303280618
582261LV00001B/8/P